the poet's world

Rita Dove on the balcony outside the Poetry Office at the Library of Congress, 1994. Photo by Fred Viebahn.

Rita Dove

Poet Laureate Consultant in Poetry 1993-95

the poet's world

LIBRARY OF CONGRESS   WASHINGTON   1995

This publication of two lectures delivered by Rita Dove at the
Library of Congress on May 5 and October 6, 1994, is supported
by the Gertrude Clarke Whittall Poetry and Literature Fund,
the Center for the Book Fund, and the Verner W. Clapp Publication Fund.

Library of Congress Cataloging-in-Publication Data

Dove, Rita.
  The poet's world / Rita Dove.
    p. cm.
  Includes bibliographical references.
  ISBN 0-8444-0874-3
  1. Dove, Rita—Aesthetics. 2. Women poets, American—20th
century—Biography. 3. Dove, Rita—Biography. 4. Poetry.
I. Title.
PS3554.0884Z468   1995
811'.54—dc20   95-5323
[B]   CIP

This publication is printed on acid-free paper.

Cover photo: Rita Dove on the porch of her cabin—where she writes—
in Charlottesville, Virginia, 1995. Photo by Fred Viebahn.

Design and composition by Adrianne Onderdonk Dudden

contents

Rita Dove at the University of Virginia with fifth-graders from Albemarle County. Photo by Michael Marshall.

preface

An aspect of the Poet Laureate's statutory duties is to deliver a lecture at either the beginning or the end of the literary year. Rita Dove chose to close the 1993-94 year with a lecture and to begin the 1994-95 year with a second, conceiving of the two as an address to a single theme. She spoke of the double vision from the poet's house, looking out to the world beyond the front and back doors and also within the house to her own creative experience. The coherence of the two lectures enables us to publish them together in this small volume, which marks also the reinstitution of the former practice of publishing the Consultant in Poetry's lectures, signaled in 1993 when (after a lapse since 1984) we printed Mona van Duyn's *Matters of Poetry*.

The illustrations in this booklet capture some of the varied places and activities energized by Rita during the past year and one-half. Most of the enlivening photographs are by Rita's husband, Fred Viebahn, a gifted photographer as well as novelist. The images can only suggest in their still state the vitality and warmth that Rita brings to her manifold projects as Poet Laureate. Whether it was celebrating "Lady Freedom among Us" when the statue of Freedom returned refurbished to the top of the Capitol, or discussing with Bill Moyers the desirability of making feelings accessible through poetry, Rita has brought new audiences to poetry and new poetry to familiar audiences.

Through imaginative programming, she has revealed poetry's evocative power when combined with jazz or when built upon the traditional love of their land by Crow Indian teenagers.

This volume becomes thus a token of poetic energy and insight, one aspect of two years full of the demonstrated possibilities of reclaiming ground for that written and spoken condensate called poetry.

Prosser Gifford
Director of Scholarly Programs
November 28, 1994

lady freedom among us

Statue of Freedom in front of the U.S. Capitol, 1993. Courtesy of the Architect of the Capitol.

don't lower your eyes
or stare straight ahead to where
you think you ought to be going

don't mutter *oh no*
not another one
get a job fly a kite
go bury a bone

with her oldfashioned sandals
with her leaden skirts
with her stained cheeks and whiskers and heaped up trinkets
she has risen among us in blunt reproach

she has fitted her hair under a hand-me-down cap
and spruced it up with feathers and stars

slung over one shoulder she bears
the rainbowed layers of charity and murmurs
all of you   even the least of you

don't cross to the other side of the square
don't think *another item to fit on a tourist's agenda*

consider her drenched gaze her shining brow
she who has brought mercy back into the streets
and will not retire politely to the potter's field

having assumed the thick skin of this town
its gritted exhaust its sunscorch and blear
she rests in her weathered plumage
bigboned   resolute

don't think you can ever forget her
don't even try
she's not going to budge
no choice but to grant her space
crown her with sky
for she is one of the many
and she is each of us

stepping out
the poet in the world

The world is too much with us; late and soon,
Getting and spending, we lay waste our powers:
Little we see in Nature that is ours.
—William Wordsworth (1807)

A room is a place where you hide from the wolves
outside and that's all any room is.
—Jean Rhys, *Good Morning, Midnight* (1939)

Rita Dove at home in Charlottesville, Virginia, 1994. Photo by Fred Viebahn.

part 1 **house and yard**

". . . The houses that were lost forever continue to live on in us," says Gaston Bachelard in his exemplary book *The Poetics of Space* (p. 56). This quote itself has "lived on" in me since I first stumbled across it as an anxious and quite Romantic (with a capital R!) graduate student. That is, on the surface I promptly forgot this particular statement, eschewing its simplicity for the more esoteric passages in the book which revolved around terms like *phenomenology, transsubjectivity*, and *ontology*.

But maybe I had to forget—no, sublimate—it so that the essence of the quote would live on in me, generating a kind of poetic consciousness of occupied space—of the space we inhabit, of the shape of thought and the pressure of absence. All of my books but one bear titles concerned with matters of definable space—*The Yellow House on the Corner* is wistfully specific; *Museum* evokes that specially prepared space for contemplation of significant achievements of the past. Although *Thomas and Beulah* is not a place, the two names establish a condition—these two protagonists are to be regarded as a unit, the title seems to say, a unit that becomes irrevocably wedded to a defined and also *confined* place, Akron, Ohio—much in the same way other famous moniker-teams evoke specific milieus—Barnum and Bailey, Sacco and Vanzetti, Frankie and Johnnie, Jack and Jill, Liz and Richard, Adam and Eve. The title of my collection of short fiction, *Fifth Sunday*, does a similar thing by calling attention to the aberration in the normal run of days in the week—since a month with five Sundays is a break with the ordinary, the fifth Sunday is automatically imbued with a metaphysical and moral significance. My novel *Through the Ivory Gate* connotes a place that exists in order to be moved through; it is a passage, transient space. And the title of my verse drama, *The Darker Face of the Earth*, finally locates us in the beyond, since to see the face of the earth implies a distance, and estrangement, from our world.

I once tried out a startling writing assignment on a group of graduate students. I say "startling" because I didn't know exactly what I intended to do with the computer paper and 100-count carton of Crayola crayons I had packed in my briefcase the night before until I was standing before the class. And it was startling because the exercise was so effective, and its implications have continued to intrigue me. First, I told the students to clear their desks. After they had recovered from the shock—was it possible that their creative writing professor was talking to them like an elementary school teacher?—and complied, I passed out the computer paper with the perforations still attached, one sheet per student. Then I broke open a brand-new carton of crayons—in my opinion, certainly one of the symbols of pleasurable magic in our age—and told them to pick one crayon, pass the carton on, and continue passing the box around in this manner until it was empty. And then? With their bewildered, expectant gazes upon me, Gaston Bachelard rose to the surface. "Please draw the place that immediately comes to mind at the word *home*," I said, sat down, and refused any further discussion.

They began to color, exchanging crayons and cursing the perforated edges, which I would not let them remove; some asked for a fresh sheet of paper in order to start over, a request I also refused. But soon I realized that I had never seen them so excited before. After twenty minutes, I told them to take a deep breath, turn the paper over, and draw the place they were living in now. The instruction to take a deep breath was necessary, since they looked up as if they had just had their breath knocked out of them; even the married students, those with actual houses and households and backyards instead of dorm rooms, suddenly seemed bereft. The last ten minutes of class were silent as they sketched the obligatory domicile.

What had I wanted to achieve with this exercise? If pressed to justify it before the Student Grievances Committee, I could come up with a multitude of fancy explanations and interpretations: the breaking down of sophisticated stances through the use of crayons to conjure a direct line to childhood and thus to the playful aspect of imagination; the framework of technological efficiency (that is, the printer tractor strips) as an imperative to make the drawing—i.e., the interior space—as resonant as possible. But the simple truth was that the forgotten house had risen again in me.

Any effective assignment forces you to go where you might have been too lazy, or frightened, to go before; but this time I did not give them a direct writing assignment. All I did, at the very end of the session, was to tell the class to take the pictures home and live with them for a week.

Only two or three of the students in that seminar went on to write poems about their homes or houses, but for some, a barrier had been broken, a threshold crossed, because a lot of poems about a lot of scary things began to evolve from the exercise. Try it: take a house, a space, a moment, and live with it for a week, and in all likelihood nothing will be the same again. To inhabit space with thought is analogous to the notion that language is a house we inhabit—a poet is someone who explores those spaces of sensual apprehension made inhabitable by vocabulary and syntax. No one has expressed this better than, again, Gaston Bachelard in *The Poetics of Space*:

Words—I often imagine this—are little houses, each with its cellar and garret. Commonsense lives on the ground floor, always ready to engage in "foreign commerce," on the same level as the others, as the passers-by, who are never dreamers. To go upstairs in the word house, is to withdraw, step by step; while to go down to the cellar is to dream, it is losing oneself in the distant corridors of an obscure etymology, looking for treasures that cannot be found in words. To mount and descend in the words themselves— this is a poet's life. To mount too high or descend too low, is allowed in the case of poets, who bring earth and sky together. (P. 147)

Each poem has its house of sound, its own geographical reverberations. And we could analyze poets for their preferences in domiciles, linguistically speaking: how, in her last poems, Anne Sexton traded in her cellar, complete with its Freudian guilt and the rat gnawing inside her, for the horizontal movement of her last book, *The Awful Rowing Towards God*; remember, though, that that book ends with Anne still rowing—suggesting that the yawning depths of the sea (another kind of cellar) were waiting for her skimming hope to tire. Or consider the extreme verticality of Sylvia Plath, from stars to brimstone in "The Church and the Yew Tree," or the terrifying shroud of Lady Lazarus who claims to "eat men like air." Rather than say that Plath inhabited staircases, I imagine her in a Manhattan elevator, with all the thrilling dread of the attendant drops and lifts of the stomach. Then there are Theodore Roethke's greenhouses, Lucille Clifton's kitchens, Richard Hugo's Western roadside taverns, Elizabeth Bishop's inscrutable childhood houses or, later, her adult bedrooms, snug and secure interiors in the face of Brazilian electrical storms.

I'm afraid I must postpone this train of inquiry, however, until the fall of this year, when I will present part 2 of this lecture, which bears the title: "'A Handful of Inwardness': The World in the Poet." Instead, tonight I want to explore the dynamics of inside versus outside in some contemporary American poetry—or, to put it in the more provocative form of a question: Do we, as poets, peer through a window at the world or do we step out to meet it? Do we, as poets, contemplate the universe in the embers burning on the hearth or are we reporting from the front lines, returning to the homefires only to dry out our rain-soaked and mud-splattered cloaks?

I hope you will forgive me if I start with—and often revisit—my own work for this inquiry. Although I deliberately try to remain ignorant about my own creative processes—it's one way to keep the left side of the brain from colonizing the right side, so that the poems can work in darkness, like seeds—occasionally an imperative comes from the outside, a request for a lecture, for example, which forces me to consider my own writing in a quasi-objective manner. And so I begin to analyze what is important, in my mind, to the writing process. This time, the imperative of this lecture tempted me to consider what I had long kept conveniently submerged—the realization that I was fascinated by occupied space; I was tempted and then pushed, like my students drawing their dreams of a home, to go where I had been too frightened to go before.

I began by leafing through my books, manuscripts in progress, and old notebooks. Soon I made an unsettling discovery. I realized that quite a number of my poems take place in backyards. When the backyard is not explicitly present in the poem, it is implied; even in poems set in foreign landscapes, I remembered that while writing the poem I had imagined myself—or the persona in the poem—either to be standing behind a house, or to be looking through a window at a yard.

The backyard that figures most prominently in my work is the one behind my parents' house, the yard I could go into at any time as a child without supervision, where the outside was

safe—where, as luck would have it, my father had established a
vegetable garden at which he'd toil all spring and summer, until
his Cherokee blood betrayed him by August, turning his face,
forearms, and shins an angry brick color. The ground was most-
ly clay, and rocks materialized right in the middle of the bean
rows—so he'd curse and rent powered plows and talk to the
tomatoes. Father, garden, the backyard of the world—what po-
et could resist that matrix? In fact, the problem was to let the
setting speak for itself, not to get heavy-handed with biblical im-
agery:

ADOLESCENCE—III

With Dad gone, Mom and I worked
The dusky rows of tomatoes.
As they glowed orange in sunlight
And rotted in shadow, I too
Grew orange and softer, swelling out
Starched cotton slips.

The texture of twilight made me think of
Lengths of Dotted Swiss. In my room
I wrapped scarred knees in dresses
That once went to big-band dances;
I baptized my earlobes with rosewater.
Along the window sill, the lipstick stubs
Glittered in their steel shells.

Looking out at the rows of clay
And chicken manure, I dreamed how it would happen:
He would meet me by the blue spruce,
A carnation over his heart, saying,
"I have come for you, Madam;
I have loved you in my dreams."
At his touch, the scabs would fall away.

Over his shoulder, I see my father coming toward us:
He carries his tears in a bowl,
And blood hangs in the pine-soaked air.

Thus my backyard emerges as a place for confrontation. All the required elements of a psychic landscape—comfort and loss, suffocation and risk—come together in the struggle of enclosure versus exposure.

The back door is the door of childhood. Countless movies and TV sitcoms have exploited the real-life possibilities of this symbolism. A slamming screen door signals the child's defiance of parents and the adult world—what child hasn't run out the back door in tears, vowing to go away and never come back and then they'll be sorry? And the vista from the backyard is also many children's first—albeit sheltered and contained—vision of a larger world to explore. They can catch a glimpse of the possibilities of the Open:

GEOMETRY

I prove a theorem and the house expands:
The windows jerk free to hover near the ceiling,
the ceiling floats away with a sigh.

As the walls clear themselves of everything
but transparency, the scent of carnations
leaves with them. I am out in the open

and above the windows have hinged into butterflies,
sunlight glinting where they've intersected.
They are going to some point true and unproven.

In my childhood there was also a side yard. Since it bordered on the backyard, it was considered part of it; however, it also linked up with the front yard, and together they ran into the sidewalk, that demilitarized zone right before the warning swaths of public grass which every kid in our neighborhood knew as the "devilstrip"—then came the final perilous territory of the street. This side lot was a transitional space between front and back. In early poems I ventured only as far as the back half of the side yard; but years later, long after I had managed to leave that backyard physically, I still returned, much like Beauty from the fairy tale, looking into my magic mirror to see the effect of my abandoning the garden:

A FATHER OUT WALKING ON THE LAWN

Five rings light your approach across
the dark. You're lonely, anyone

can tell—so many of you
trembling, at the center the thick

dark root. Out here on a lawn
twenty-one years
gone under the haunches of a neighbor's

house, American Beauties
lining a driveway the mirror image of your own,

you wander, waiting to be
discovered. What
can I say to a body
that merely looks

like you? The willow, infatuated with its
surroundings, quakes; not that violent
orgasm nor the vain promise of

a rose relinquishing
its famous scent all for you, no,

not even the single
brilliant feather

a blue jay loses in light
which dangles momentarily, azure scimitar,
above the warm eaves of your house—
nothing can change

this travesty, this
magician's skew of scarves
issuing from an opaque heart.

Who sees you anyway, except
at night, and with a fantastic eye?

If only you were bright enough to touch!

In this poem I have finally taken the forward half of the side yard into view; the father "out walking" at night is fully exposed—exposed, as it were, from the vantage point of the poet *who is standing in the street*.

⟁

"In the domain of values," Gaston Bachelard says, "a key closes more often than it opens, whereas the doorknob opens more often than it closes. And the gesture of closing is always sharper, firmer and briefer than that of opening" (p. 73). When one uses the back door, one *pushes* the obstruction (i.e., the door or screen) *forward* and steps out. As with a screen door, the opening is effortless—in fact, the barrier between exterior and interior is nearly illusory, a gray space: already one can see the outdoors, darkened and vague through the checkered wire-hatching, and smell the smells of freshly mown grass, hear the "sh-sh-sh" of lawn sprinklers and the "craw craw" of the raucous cicada—the exterior sensations filter into the interior space, taking up residence in one's storehouse of memories, becoming *recollections* of the outside. This sets up in me a peculiar state, one in which I am in two places at once and yet, curiously, not there at all. It is the moment of ultimate possibility, and of ultimate irresponsibility. Of course there is no absolute demarcation of the moment when *in* becomes *out*; indeed, one passes through a delicious sliding moment when one is *neither* in nor out but *floating*, suspended above the interior and exterior ground.

FIVE ELEPHANTS

are walking towards me.
When morning is still a frozen
tear in the brain, they come
from the east, trunk to tail,
clumsy ballerinas.

How to tell them all evening
I refused consolation? Five umbrellas, five
willows, five bridges and their shadows!
They lift their trunks, hooking the sky
I would rush into, split

pod of quartz and lemon. I could say
they are five memories, but
that would be unfair.
Rather pebbles seeking refuge in the heart.
They move past me. I turn and follow,

and for hours we meet no one else.

The front door, on the other hand, is a door of final exits. It is the threshold of propriety and solicitation. This is the door we imagine when John Donne speaks of the twin compass in his poem "A Valediction: Forbidding Mourning," of the wife who stays home—"the fixt foot"—and the husband who "far doth rome," who goes off in spite of the knowledge that "Moving of th' earth brings harmes and feares." Adrienne Rich, in her poem of the same title, locates the fear and loss in both the exterior landscape—the world—and the interior landscape, which is represented by language:

> A last attempt: the language is a dialect called metaphor.
> These images go unglossed: hair, glacier, flashlight.
> When I think of a landscape I am thinking of a time.
> When I talk of taking a trip I mean forever.
>
>   ("A Valediction Forbidding Mourning")

The front door opens onto the world of commerce. When you exit through the front door of your family home, you are saying goodbye to a womb, you are about to sell yourself to the world. The wind that meets you is chilly.

Why is this? Even the house interior anticipates our reception into the world. Back doors come from the kitchen; front doors open into parlors, living rooms—where, in the fifties, children were not allowed to dwell and where the sofas often were covered with thick plastic, kept new for no apparent occasion until they had gone out of style. Living room furniture was protected from wear and tear as if it were meant to endure forever, the proud owners insisting on long-lasting interior values while the world outside, sometimes even the outside of the house itself, due to neglect, went from decrepit to dangerous. Fear lies in wait outside the front door. As Henry Pussycat in John Berryman's forty-sixth "Dream Song" says, "outside"—

. . . . Incredible panic rules.
People are blowing and beating each other without mercy.
Drinks are boiling. Iced
drinks are boiling. The worse anyone feels, the worse
treated he is. Fools elect fools.
A harmless man at an intersection said, under his breath:
"Christ!"

Bad news arrives by telegram. Neighbors watching from the
street witness incriminating domestic indiscretions. Death me-
anders through the streets while we crouch behind our front
doors, in retreat. In "Boccaccio: The Plague Years," a poem from
my second book, *Museum*, Boccaccio sees each doorstep with "a
dish burning sweet / clotted smoke," a desperate incense in-
tended to protect the inhabitants of the house from succumb-
ing to the sickness; from his viewpoint behind the glass, Boc-
caccio watches "the priests sweep past / in their peaked hoods,
collecting death." And in the companion poem, "Fiammetta
Breaks Her Peace," which is about Boccaccio's idealized love,
Fiammetta ends by saying:

All is infection, mother—and avarice,
and self-pity, and fear!
we shall sit quietly in this room
and I think we'll be spared.

Fear enters the house. Fear is let in when we open the door,
whether we step out or just look out to see what's going on in
the streets. What does it help to keep the door locked if you
venture outside for a breath of fresh air, a bit of life? Can you
count on making it back inside? In his novel *Chronicle of a Death
Foretold*, Gabriel García Márquez has his protagonist hacked to
death on the threshold of his mother's house; his death is made
all the more horrifying by the fact that his mother, believing her

son to be upstairs, locks the door a second before he gains the safety of entrance—which allows his pursuers the luxury of a thorough butchery. What horror!—to be locked out by one's mother, to run back trying to escape the world's treachery and not be permitted back inside. This ultimate terror is expressed by the Lebanese poet Nadia Tuéni in Willis Barnstone's translation:

Nothing but a man
let's execute him against the door.
The morning of taking him away was robed
    with the freshness of water;
it would be best to finish him off
    against a door of blue wood.

Now, in the back of the house we have the kitchen, with the warmth of the hearth. The kitchen is a place for conversation, for social intercourse, for oral history; a place to return to again and again, a place where the daughter, home from the wide world, can join her mother as I did in my poem "In the Old Neighborhood" and "Lean at the sink, listen to her chatter / while the pressure cooker ticks / *whole again whole again now.*"

American women have traditionally used the back or kitchen door as the exit and entrance when conducting neighborly transactions. Remember the TV series "Mary Hartman, Mary Hartman"? What was so charming about that offbeat soap opera was that it treated suburban American life at once at face value and *ad absurdum*, so that ordinary movements were multiplied into surreal motifs; Mary Hartman existed in her sunny kitchen, and news of the world entered through the back door; neighbors came by to borrow sugar and drop off gossipy bombshells; husband Tom came home from work and breezed through the kitchen to that front room we never got to see in order to watch TV—thus effectively cutting himself off from Mary; the children trooped in for cookies and milk, airing their grievances.

When a woman leaves the kitchen through the back door, she retains the interior life—that handful of intimacy—even while she moves away from her own mother's life: "I walk out the kitchen door / trailing extension cords into the open / gaze of the southwest," begins my poem "The Other Side of the House," the first poem in a seven-part sequence which examines the perimeters of new motherhood. Significantly, the sequence found its inspiration in the backyard of my and my husband's first own house; elsewhere, in an essay titled "The House That Jill Built," I have described how I and a photographer friend, also a professor and mother, spent weeks drinking coffee in that same backyard as we searched for a theme for a collaborative project—only to discover that we were sitting right in the middle of it, that the project had to involve this backyard where "curls of evaporated gasoline" floated from the lawnmower, a backyard where "the hinged ax of the butterfly pauses."

Then there are porches—those dinosaurs of a seemingly more sociable age. Have you noticed how forlorn a house looks without a front porch? Have you noticed that nowadays it is a mark of affluence to have a front porch that one does not use? I believe that porches must be inhabited to be of positive influence on our consciousness—otherwise, they exude the bereft melancholy of an abandoned nest. Porches can also serve as halfway houses—for the elderly a porch is the airlock between the world, which they are too frail to negotiate, and the prison of confined convalescence. Like the shadowy twilight of Virgil's Underworld, the screen porch with its occupied rocking chair is the halfway house between the World and the Afterworld. In Maxine Kumin's poem "The Porch Swing," a brother and sister go out to the porch during a family reunion to ". . . look death straight / in its porcelain teeth, daring it / to squeeze onto the porch swing / where we rock away half a century." And the boundary between the familiar circle of the family and the cold air of the future is felt keenly in Philip Levine's poem "Starlight," which begins:

> My father stands in the warm evening
> on the porch of my first house.
> I am four years old and growing tired.

The poet reconstructs the memory from a four-year-old's perspective; we see his father's head "among the stars, / the glow of his cigarette, redder / than the summer moon." Then the boy asks his father if he is happy, but even though the father nods in the affirmative, his gestures—his very being—suggest that he's lying. In an instant, the comfort of house and summer dissipate to reveal the real scene. Instead of father and son, the poet shows us:

> a tall, gaunt child
> holding his child against the promises
> of autumn, until the boy slept
> never to waken in that world again.

The stoop, on the other hand, is a public place. It is at turns a soapbox for airing opinion and an eagle's aerie, a lookout post. It is, in fact, the urban equivalent to the kitchen, with its warm and comforting talk, though it is usually occupied by the young. (In the urban scenario, women remain in the apartments, while the elderly occupy streetside windows instead of porches.)

Portions of the house have served as metaphors for the seat of creativity itself. Philip Levine's poem "The House" begins:

This poem has a door, a locked door,
and windows drawn against the day,
but at night lights come on, one
in each room, and the neighbors swear
they hear music and the sound of dancing.
These days the neighbors will swear
to anything.

In her poem "Locked Doors," Anne Sexton describes a heaven "up there / with an iron door that can't be opened. / It has all your bad dreams in it"; as much as she would like to "turn the rusty key," she "can only sit here on earth / at [her] place at the table." In Gregory Orr's brief poem "The Room," the speaker first draws a room, then enters it, finally crawling through the picture of a window he also has drawn and held against the wall. Though he walks away, he still carries the room within him: "I saw the lights / of a village," he reports, ". . . and always, at my back, I felt / the white room swallowing what was passed."

We cannot talk about front and back doors, porches and front stoops and kitchens, without considering the role of these domestic topographies in light of the concepts of racial privilege. Historically, the back door was assigned to children and servants. Subordinates use back entrances; in Richard Wright's *Native Son* we know that Bigger Thomas is doomed from the moment he chooses to ring at the front door of his new (white) employers' mansion, and we know that his white employers will be implicitly guilty in Bigger's crime when they *allow* him to enter through the front door.

In the skewed order of racial privilege, a black person's "proper place" used to be the back—of the bus, the movie theater, and the house. "Oh, wash-woman," Langston Hughes exclaims: "Was it four o'clock or six o'clock on a winter afternoon, / I saw you wringing out the last shirt in Miss White / Lady's kitchen?" And whereas the black protagonist of another Langston Hughes poem, "I, too, sing America," confidently proclaims when "sent to eat in the kitchen": "But I laugh, and eat well, / and grow strong" for the day "when they'll see how beautiful I am / And be ashamed," the speaker in Melvin B. Tolson's epic poem "Harlem Gallery" is more impatient:

> Black Boy,
> let me get up from the white man's Table of Fifty Sounds
> in the kitchen; let me gather the crumbs and cracklings
> of this autobio-fragment,
> before the curtain with the skull and bones descends.

If a particular segment of society has been confined to a discriminatory domain, its members will strive to get out of it or in some way transform their surroundings. The back entrance, and that real estate around it, becomes an object of shame: in an early Gwendolyn Brooks poem ("a song in the front yard"), a little girl who is being raised "properly" complains about being kept in the front yard all her life; she wants "a peek at the back / Where it's rough and untended and hungry weed grows." Her yearning for the weedy backyard is equated with her desire "to be a bad woman" like Johnnie Mae "[a]nd wear the brave stockings of night-black lace." Lucille Clifton's Aunt Rosie sits "wrapped up like garbage / . . . surrounded by the smell of too old potato peels"; in my book *Thomas and Beulah*, in the poem "Sunday Greens," the smell of cooking collard greens causes the house to stink "like a zoo in summer," until Beulah wishes for "pride to roar through / the kitchen until it shines."

Since, however, the kitchen is, spiritually speaking, the source of nourishment and intimate communion as well as the repository for folklore and affairs of the soul, to repudiate its influence is also to deny a significant aspect of one's psychological makeup. One becomes not only cut off from one's roots but estranged from one's own voice. The female or ethnic artist who eschews the kitchen completely also denies the positive anima of this spiritual domicile—its privacy and intimacy, its down-to-earth gratitudes and communal acceptance. To equate success with public recognition means that female or ethnic artists will demand to leave and enter by the front door, so long denied them. Driven by hunger, afraid to turn back in defeat, the artist hunches her shoulders and pushes further into the wind; in time, the hunch becomes a chip, and then we have the other extreme: the shrill, self-righteous protest of slogans and rap, the super-ego jargon of political correctness. One may control the streets only at the price of one's soul.

part 2   **a toe over the threshold**

It is difficult to find the Poetry and Literature Center in the Jefferson Building of the Library of Congress. Journalists and visitors invariably get lost—especially now, with ongoing renovations that require each traveler to descend to the cellar, walk a corridor hung low with pipes and ducts, finally board a padded elevator for what is called the Attic—and then, still, one must turn several unassuming corners to find the office of the Poet Laureate, tucked away on the top floor, high above the Great Hall.

One journalist questioned me about it, and his attitude surprised me. He was standing next to the French doors leading out to the massive balcony facing the Capitol when he asked, "How does it feel to be stuck up in a corner of the building like this? Do you find it symbolic of the place poetry has in our society?"

I stepped up to the glass doors and looked out—slightly to my right, the dome of the Capitol shone; behind it soared the Washington Monument, then, beyond the tufts of green and shingled roofs, I could make out the brick bastion of the Smithsonian and, in the distance, the Lincoln Memorial. He called *this* "stuck up in a corner?" It is one of the best urban views in the world!

Of course I know what he meant—madwomen in the attic, starving writer in the garret, all that. Even James Thurber stuck his dotty grandfather in a bed in the attic. But consider: in the very center of our mighty nation's seat of government, the poet stands, perched, so to speak, atop the accumulated wisdom of the centuries (all those millions of books and recordings and other artifacts of knowledge—art, manuscripts, music scores and even musical instruments!), and the poet is looking down on the lawmakers and all the symbols of dominion—for Washington is nothing if not a study in symbolic gestures. Domes and basilisks, columns and marble stairs, statuary and fountains and rosettes carved in granite niches. What a view! On second thought, it wasn't a view—it was an *overview*.

Which started me thinking: What is the setting of contemporary American poetry? Before what backdrops do today's poets, those purveyors of Keats's "Truth and Beauty," William Carlos Williams's news "for lack of which men die every day," Stevens's "palm at the end of the mind," and Marianne Moore's "place for the genuine"—before what backdrops do today's poets compose; before what backdrops are today's poems being played out?

It is a simpler and perhaps more intriguing matter to ask, "What is wrong with the picture of contemporary poetry?" than to explore what is right. What is wrong is something so basic, so essentially obvious, that at first and even second glance we don't notice it at all: American poets rarely step into the outside world. By that I mean that the poems locate their musings inside rooms, often before windows or the shaving mirror, in bars and theaters and, as I just showed you with examples from my own work, the childhood backyard. The poet ventures no further than to the compost heap out back or, when there's an exterior scene, it is often an urban landscape—like Gerald Stern strolling the streets of Manhattan.

I have conducted an experiment to test my theory about our reluctance to step out. Using an anthology of contemporary poetry which shall remain anonymous, I lifted lines at random to make a composite poem of our times:

FROM MY COUCH I RISE

Outside the window it's starting to snow;
the potted ferns lean down.

This is the best part of the evening:
the food cooking, the armchair.
Sometimes I hear her talking
as she roams from room to room.

I've lined all our wineglasses up on the sill.
I can sit for a while with a dust of flowers
in the living room and in the bedroom.

I had been looking across falling snow
but now, inside this moment,
between the cerulean panes,
the scarred desk the bookcases and books,

almost over this room
the sun is gliding.

I need some new knick-knacks
to suggest an air of cleanliness.
Ahead, a world of blue-grass lawns.

After a time I lie down on the floor
and ease into dreams,
a quilt stretched
over my knees.

I remember hiding in the hall closet
alone in the dark, listening to music.
I remember how she cried in the kitchen.

I roll over and the room moves
a little closer.

I am, of course, grossly unfair and unfairly gross. There exists an esteemed pantheon of nature poets in our midst—Mary Oliver, for instance, and Wendell Berry, Gary Snyder, Diane Ackerman. And there are poets who are grounded in real-life vocations that keep them outside much of the year—Maxine Kumin raises horses and runs a farm in New Hampshire; Donald Hall still lives on his ancestral farm, also in New Hampshire. And I am not assigning literary worth according to whether a poem's setting is rural, urban, or suburban; writing about crop cycles and the hard lessons of farm life does not make a poet more authentic or vital. I'm talking about the way poets today view themselves and their function in the world, the world that Wittgenstein says "is everything that is the case."

I'm skiing on the NordicTrac these days—after several guilty years spent enjoying it as a piece of postmodern furniture, all those Reebok commercials and the grocery shelves stocked with bottled waters, the scales at lunch counters for measuring one's meager portion of salad and my own tightening waistband finally got to me: I have crawled, huffing and puffing, onto the fitness wagon. This is not where I would like to be. I personally favor silhouettes tending to Rubenesque rather than Klimt, and a life without potato chips and desserts, in my opinion, is a diminished one. However, stress and increasing physical lethargy have led me to the waters where I steadfastly refused to drink before.

A few years after graduate school I ran into a former workshop classmate who had discovered his rhythm—he jogged. He was also a lawyer, an occupation I regard in the same way as I regard faculty meetings—a necessity, but one I'm relieved that others seem to like doing. For John, the ritual of rising with the sun, suiting up, and setting out on his prescribed route through the woods was a gentle way of nudging his synapses. Stimulated without being jarred or distracted, he said his thoughts were free to range with his eyes, the iambic pentameter of his heartbeat joined with the metric and literal footsteps, and all this regular pacing forming a matrix for the images that floated through his mind. Each morning when he got back home, he sat down and wrote—fifty pages of tercets in the end, a long meditative poem.

Jogging, however, I've always found boring and exhibitionist—I couldn't bear the thought of motorists glimpsing my dull and stunned expression, my shuddering jowls and vaguely focused eyes, wrists drooping from exhaustion and my mouth hanging dumbly. Aerobics, on the other hand, was far too perky for me—no melancholy allowed in a mirrored room with twenty other people moving their neon latexed limbs in unison. Personal tapes such as Jane Fonda's workout left me in physical therapy for weeks—it seems I've inherited an impact-sensitive hip from my mother. Yoga makes me claustrophobic; to me, emptying my mind of desire is tantamount to literary death. In general, I have always regarded sports as an extravagant waste of time, perhaps because I lack the competitive edge, and have never enjoyed losing myself in the mind-set of "team spirit." Walking? As a woman, I'd feel that I would need to find a walking partner for protection; however, the obligation of making conversation while I speedwalk through the landscape is more depressing than pumping iron in a high-fly gym echoing with grunts and the swish of ropes sliding through glistening metal pulleys.

No, I prefer to do my time alone and in full knowledge of my actions. I need low impact and some routine that doesn't last longer than a half hour, forty minutes tops. NordicTrac became my torturer of choice.

Admittedly, I feel better and have less appetite for superfluous food. Once a day I pull on my sweats, go to the basement, turn on the TV for distraction, and ski. The first five minutes are nonchalant; the next ten are always hell; and from then on it's an otherworldly experience. While skiing I watch whatever variety of entertainment the networks happen to be dishing up. I get off exhilarated, but with the pounding heart and glowing skin that tells me I have earned my dinner. But I also have acquired a random sampling of situation comedies, real-life court proceedings, sleaze masquerading as news, surreal talk shows, and maddeningly jokey "family entertainment." And one thing often strikes me: No matter what the program, I generally find myself looking into interiors—a living room or a studio kitchen, a courtroom or a jail cell. The back door swings open, and the neighbor comes in; in one teens' show, the neighborhood kid actually enters and exits his friend's room through the second-floor window, using a ladder. Outside shots—a two-second take of the house exterior or a Manhattan intersection—are flashed onscreen to signify passage of time. The larger world, then, becomes synonymous with collapsed time, while the illusion of real time occurs in carefully scripted dialogues within the sanctum of our residential cubicles. Even news programs such as "20/20" and "Inside Edition," which one might assume would feature more incidents occurring in the world, very often offer segments in which an individual's private sanctum is being set upon by the Big Bad World. During an interview, most extended scenes are interior ones; the subject's contact with the world is invariably represented by quick shots of the person walking down the driveway of his or her home, with a cut to the subject standing forlornly before the building wherein sit those who have maligned her and cast her out.

Where are we living? I find myself wondering. What do we make of the view on the other side of our windows and windshields? And if we have so little contact with that silent, greening world, what contact can we possibly have with the larger arena of life? In a society where neighbors are strangers and children are in danger if they roam the community streets, what possible significance can the term "global village" have? No wonder that we, as writers, have increasingly retreated to the assayable world of our self-made interiors: Li-Young Lee begins his poem "This Room and Everything in It" with these lines: "I am letting this room / and everything in it / stand for my ideas about love / and its difficulties." This exercise, the poet assures us, will come in handy:

> one day, when I need
> to tell myself something intelligent
> about love,
>
> I'll close my eyes
> and recall this room and everything in it.

The tautology of his argument smells suspiciously of a vicious circle, and it comes as no surprise that the next line is: "My body is estrangement." The poem disintegrates on the page, becoming a desert of ellipses as the poet attempts to recover the magic of a room after lovemaking, the *heile Welt* of desire before its completion, when all is possibility.

In his marvelous book *The Rain in the Trees*, W. S. Merwin has a poem called "The Horizons of Rooms," which begins:

> There have been rooms for such a short time
> and now we think there is nothing else unless it is raining
>
> or snowing or very late
> with everyone else in another dark room
>
> for a time beyond measure there were no rooms
> and now many have forgotten the sky

In an interview printed a few years ago in *Ms.* Magazine, Margaret Atwood states the case clearly:

> When you begin to write, you're in love with the language, with the act of creation, with yourself partly; but as you go on, the writing—if you follow it—will take you places you never intended to go and show you things you would never otherwise have seen. I began as a profoundly apolitical writer, but then I began to do what all novelists and some poets do: I began to describe the world around me.

It's not as if we don't have poets who have taken to heart Wittgenstein's statement, "The world is everything that is the case." We have Adrienne Rich and Philip Levine, Yusef Komunyakaa and Sandra Cisneros, Maxine Kumin and Stanley Kunitz, C. K. Williams and Audre Lorde, Shirley Kaufman and Stephen Dunn, Gerald Stern and Toi Derricotte, Margaret Atwood and Seamus Heaney, just for starters. But although we have our poets who speak up against the atrocities of life elsewhere—be it the Holocaust or El Salvador or past horrors in the Dominican Republic or in America's antebellum South—I wonder why we have such difficulty stepping outside our metaphorical houses and talking to our neighbor across the street. Why is it so much easier to bear witness either to our interior spaces, our interior lives, or to the life that is far away from us, the life we see reported on television or read about in books? If we can't take the immediate world around us as the case, isn't it more likely that we'll fall prey to the titillation of "safe" danger— usurping the sufferings of others to serve the purposes of our quiet literary despairs?

No, I'm not thinking of anything as blunt as political versus nonpolitical poetry; rather, I'm convinced our problem lies with the immediate dis-ease we feel whenever the words "politics" and "poetry" are uttered in the same room—the swift assumption that political plus poetical equals agitprop. The general attitude, in some halls of our "high poetry," is that the less we associate with the goings-on in the street—the quirky, messy shenanigans of daily life—the purer our art becomes.

I have spoken so much of houses because we have embodied them in one form or another in our very American psyches, even to the point that we have tried to quantify sexual harassment in terms of whether permission has been given to trespass onto designated erogenous zones; if our homes are our castles, then our bodies are assiduously maintained like the castle grounds, and we barricade our feelings to protect our hearts, which have become the castle keep.

These ideas are not new. Muriel Rukeyser said it long ago, in her poem "Then I Saw What the Calling Was," which appeared in her 1948 book *The Green Wave*:

All the voices of the wood called "Muriel!"
but it was soon solved; it was nothing, it was not for me.
The words were a little like Mortal and More and Endure
and a word like Real, a sound like Health or Hell.
Then I saw what the calling was: it was the road I traveled,
the clear
time and these colors of orchards, gold behind gold and the
full
shadow behind each tree and behind each slope. Not to me
the calling, but to anyone, and at last I saw: where
the road lay through sunlight and many voices and the
marvel
orchards, not for me, not for me, not for me.
I came into my clear being; uncalled, alive, and sure.
Nothing was speaking to me, but I offered and all was well.

And then I arrived at the powerful green hill.

Perhaps the solution is a lot more straightforward than we think. Perhaps what we contemporary American poets first must do is, as private citizens, to step out the front door and look around. Taste the air, see what is out there. Say hello to the stranger and join the community beyond the castle walls. Perhaps only then can we find the right mix between the interior moment and the pulse of the world. Perhaps when we begin to involve ourselves in the world, no matter on how local or limited a level, we will have begun to offer ourselves to the calling. Only then will we hear the resonance inside ourselves—that place Rukeyser describes as "the inner condition of the body . . . the *in*vironment"—and only then can we begin to take ourselves seriously as the kind of poets Percy Byssche Shelley calls "the unacknowledged legislators of the race." And at that point, my friends, the real work begins.

"a handful of inwardness"

the world in the poet

Die Welt ist alles, was der Fall ist.
(The world is everything that is the case.)
> —Ludwig Wittgenstein,
> *Tractatus Logico-Philosophicus*
> (1922), 1

Rita Dove at home in Charlottesville, Virginia, 1994. Photo by Fred Viebahn.

At the conclusion of the Library of Congress's 1993-94 literary season this past May, I delivered a lecture entitled "Stepping Out: The Poet in the World." Not only did I discuss the significance of place in contemporary poetry—the *ur*-comfort of kitchens and *ur*-terror of basements, the metaphysical thresholds of back doors and transitional spaces of porch and front stoop—but I also commented upon the seeming reluctance of many Americans to leave their living rooms and the corresponding qualms of many contemporary American poets to become engaged with the outside world, to open the front door of the castle keep and step into life. I did not exempt my own poetry from this inquiry, noting my predilection for titles that refer to houses and other edifices, as well as poems featuring backyards, neighborhood streets, and domestic interiors. I also shared with you one of my favorite passages from a book called *The Poetics of Space,* by French phenomenologist Gaston Bachelard:

> Words—I often imagine this—are little houses, each with its cellar and garret. Commonsense lives on the ground floor, always ready to engage in "foreign commerce," on the same level as the others, as the passers-by, who are never dreamers. To go upstairs in the word house, is to withdraw, step by step; while to go down to the cellar is to dream, it is losing oneself in the distant corridors of an obscure etymology, looking for treasures that cannot be found in

words. To mount and descend in the words themselves—this is a poet's life.

And last May I promised to pursue that train of thought—actually, that ladder of thought—by opening the 1994-95 season with a sequel to "Stepping Out." I've called my lecture this evening "'A Handful of Inwardness': The World in the Poet"—a title that's derived from a line in a poem by Rainer Maria Rilke, the poem "A Bowl of Roses," which I will discuss later.

First, however, let me mention that a little something happened since last we met, which has provoked a slightly different introduction to this topic than I had originally intended. A little something called *My Summer Vacation.*

No, I am not about to make a disclaimer. We'll merely be taking a small detour, a personal tangent by which I hope to illustrate Bachelard's ingenious analogy while preparing us for tonight's central theme: the need for the intimate and private in poetry, and the ways in which poetry reaches out while turning inward.

When the first reporter posed the question how I felt about being asked to serve as Poet Laureate, I unwisely blurted out, "It'll ruin my life, but I'd be crazy not to accept it." I've been called on the carpet for that remark more than once—by those who thought me ungracious and ungrateful, by those who believed accepting any position even remotely affiliated with government meant selling out and therefore couldn't understand why not accepting the appointment would be crazy, by those who thought my publicized worries were mere coquetry, since such a title could only further my career. But I had just one meaning in mind when making that comment: Accepting the duties and the accompanying public exposure of the Laureateship would wreak havoc with my writing life. By the same token, to refuse the challenge of promoting poetry from this vantage point and position of visibility would be to abdicate my responsibility as a humanist, an educator, and, yes, an artist. To turn my back would mean, for my own conscience at least, that I would no longer have the moral right to complain about lack of funding for literature, or the state of the humanities in our schools, or even the fate of poetry in the hands of commercial publishing. And so I had to take up this gauntlet cast at my feet. I was offered a chance to do something about the state of poetry in our country, to increase the public profile for the arts, and any little bit of progress made might result in a larger audience for all poetry and a more hospitable environment for the arts.

During my first year in this post it was gratifying to see confirmed my steadfast belief that there is a much greater hunger for poetry than book sales and reading attendances usually indicate. But I was forced to accept what I had feared from the start would happen: I wasn't writing. No poetry, or too little poetry. There simply was no time. No real time, no quiet time in which to "mount and descend in the words themselves."

So after a year of reeling through events and appearances, a year of being a full-time public person (and sometimes feeling like public property), this summer I fled to where phone and fax could not find me—an old stone house in a small village in southern France, a village famous for nothing, with no tourists, shopping centers, or distractions. My husband and I had rented the place sight unseen, through American friends who own a house there. Our place belonged to a London stage designer. The first thing that confronted us upon opening the eight-foot wooden door with a key as big and rusty as a jailer's was a flight of stone stairs where, at the top step under the corner, a spider so large its legs seemed to be pleated, hurriedly retreated into a crumbling hole. Another set of wooden doors led down the dark central corridor to the living room, which had an Addams Family type of grandeur, thanks to huge mirrors leaning precariously against the walls, faded Persian carpets, a battalion of makeshift sofas and armchairs draped in chenille spreads and white sheets. There were fringes on lampshades, a large white-washed fireplace, and candles everywhere—six-foot candelabras with thick white candles screwed onto iron filigree posts, green candles leaning in wine bottles lined up atop the cavernous hearth in the kitchen, purple candles stuck in flowerpots on the grotto-like terrace.

As a theater designer, the owner obviously had scavenged props after productions were over. A huge stone head of a visored warrior stared balefully at me as I worked—he rested in the top of a three-foot vase painted with red and silver griffins. A stone eagle resided over the sideboard, one wing spread above my portable printer—the other wing lay broken behind him. But no object was what it seemed: That warrior head was actually feather-light, made from Styrofoam painted gray, and the eagle was cast from plaster. An elaborate Chinese vase turned out to be made of papier-mâché, what looked like giant pincushions mounted over the mantel was actually a collection of needle-point footstool covers. The house could have served as a stage set itself; and for a proscenium arch, in the living room was a tall window, looking out over the vineyards to where the remains of a nineteenth-century castle sprawled halfway up the hills, dun-colored against the dusty green.

However, this stage set hosted a few unwanted cast members. The first evening I walked into the kitchen—that ancient haven for gossip and nourishment—and discovered in the sink a frightening specimen of local fauna, dark red and two inches long, with distinctive curved arms like a saguaro cactus or a man in distress: a scorpion. I'd never seen a scorpion this size, and even in my panicked denial marveled at how symmetrical it was, how undeniably itself.

Don't worry, our American friends assured us, the scorpions, at least the dark ones, were not too poisonous—"more like a wasp's sting." Anyway, most of the scorpions were dead by the time you saw them, because the millipedes killed them.

Millipedes? I recognized the hint of hysteria in my voice and stopped, proposing a silent détente: Insects, don't show yourselves, and I won't look. I wanted desperately to like this place; I needed to write.

In my earlier lecture I spoke about the spaces our imagination occupies and how our houses correspond to them. In a temporary rental situation like ours, two weeks in a house we'd never seen before, two weeks wherein we hoped to write, the strange new physical space and the mind must develop alliances that provoke imagination and creation. Absorbing details and for a while becoming a hybrid of the person you've known and a person you've dreamed about, you begin to occupy new territory.

We immediately went on a night schedule. I've been a night person all my life—by that I mean that I naturally become more animated after dusk, and if left to my own resources would work until dawn—but I had rarely been able to commit to a full-fledged night life since becoming a teacher and becoming a mother, both of which had urged more and more of a daylight schedule on me. But now, in this surrogate shelter, I wrote until the cock crowed, then read in bed until 8:00 or 9:00 A.M., then slept the scorching hours of the afternoon away, often having breakfast as "late" as 4:00 or 5:00 P.M. Brief forays into the countryside were made just before twilight, with dinner happening around nine or ten in the evening.

After the dishes were washed and the heavy old fan lugged from kitchen to living room, after plugging in the electric Neocide insect repellent dispenser to fend off the bugs which ventured through the open window, I sat down at my table and waited. Waited for what? Not for inspiration, not quite—as the composer Ned Rorem said, "One only gets what one puts into one's miracles."

I will never know exactly how or why writing happens. For every spurt of creativity, there are interminable stretches of drudgery, accompanied by an endless supply of ordinary, lifeless words. Every evening I'd search for distraction, but there was no television, and my fear of Scorpions & Company—whose ranks now included one small, adroit bat up in the third-floor studio where my husband worked—kept me in my seat. So I sat and waited until my mind grew tired of running around in circles and started to dream. When the mind dreams, it whispers . . . inaudibly at first, and then—if you don't frighten it with too close or judgmental a scrutiny—comes a clear and steady stream of near-words. I am convinced that the voice some writers refer to when describing inspiration is nothing less than the mind talking in its dreams.

So, finally, I was ready to move into Bachelard's word house. There were nights when I worked three hours on a single line, only to write two poems immediately after that line suddenly righted itself. One evening I gave myself leave to goof off, since the night before I had finished a reasonable draft of a long poem that had been stalled for over three years; I did two crossword puzzles, read a trashy British novel found in the spare bedroom and finally, bored witless, started to work on this lecture—but instead a poem burst out in less than thirty minutes, a poem I had had no inkling of before sitting down at the desk. I believe the poem came so easily because I had been working with such concentration and continuity, for days on end. I was actually living language—which is to say, language was no longer a commodity to be traded but had become a reality to be lived out, a reality where, as Bachelard says, "A word is a bud attempting to become a twig."

But at what cost came those two weeks of incredible productivity! We traveled to one of the most beautiful and desirable corners of Europe, only to board ourselves up in an old house and write. We didn't see Avignon or walk the streets of Cannes. We never even made it to the church at St. Guilhem le Désert, a mere fifteen miles away, one of the world's most beautiful Romanesque buildings. So out of sync with normal commerce were we that, two nights before our departure when acquaintances on their way from Barcelona to Paris dropped by and began talking about what had happened in the United States in the last few weeks, I developed a nervous sore throat!

I think that I could not have stood many more days in that house, just as I believe that those were two of the most remarkable weeks in my life. I simply could not have borne up under such isolated intensity for much longer.

⤠

Admittedly, my summer vacation experience was at direct odds with the challenge I issued in last May's lecture when I posed this question: "Do we American poets peer through a window at the world, or do we step out to meet it?" Perhaps a more useful set of questions would be: What windows do we choose to look out of—or into? What of the world do we see when we look . . . and if we do step out, what do we carry with us?

In Rainer Maria Rilke's poem "Die Rosenschale" (translated as "The Bowl of Roses" by Edward Snow), the narrator witnesses, from his window, a neighborhood fight. He has seen

> two boys
> ball themselves up into something
> that was pure hatred, rolling on the ground
> like an animal attacked by bees;
> actors, towering exaggerators,
> raging horses crashing down,
> casting their gaze away, baring their teeth
> as if their mouths were peeling from their skulls . . . .

He turns from this exhibition of extravagant violence to contemplate the quintessential Romantic symbol of lyric poetry:

before you stands this full bowl of roses,
which is unforgettable, and filled to the brim
with that utmost of being and bending,
offering up, lacking power to give, standing here,
that might be ours.

The opportunities for self-indulgence and preciousness clamor on all sides, but Rilke threads his way through the minefield of romanticism to the very crux of his inquiry. First he considers this "Noiseless life, endless opening out, / space being used, without space being taken"; then he ponders the feeling that arises in himself, a "pure within-ness, so much strange tenderness / and self-illumination—out to the very edge." He anticipates our postmodern cynicism, admitting that it is not the beauty of the rose that moves us to wonder, but rather the fact that we, jaded creatures with our contemporary angst, are moved in spite of our skepticism: We are surprised that we are still capable of awe in the face of beauty: "is somewhere something known to us like this?" he asks, "that a feeling arises, / because flower petals touch flower petals?"

Unembarrassed, Rilke proceeds to examine the roses in detail—slowing us down, persuading us to turn our gaze from the angers of the street by reacquainting ourselves with the felicitous satisfactions of paying close and tender attention, each translucent petal and tangled stamen, from a blissful white rose to

. . . that blushing one, which turns around
as if embarrassed to one that's cool,
and how the cool one unfeelingly withdraws,
and how that cold one stands, wrapped in itself,
among the open ones, which are shedding everything.

Of course, the roses stand for our various postures of flawed humanity. But Rilke doesn't stop there—beyond Romanticism, he proceeds to the rhetorical question: "What can't they be?" His roses can be everything in the world, since they are the lens of our contemplation, not its intent or desire.

And so the poem concludes:

> And aren't all that way: simply self-containing,
> if self-containing means: to transform the world outside
> and the wind and the rain and the patience of spring
> and guilt and restlessness and muffled fate
> and even the changing and flying and fleeing of the clouds
> and the vague influence of the distant stars
> into a handful of inwardness.

> It now lies carefree in these open roses.

With a single breathless sentence, Rilke returns us from a trip around the world where, like Doktor Faustus, we have witnessed its terrors and injustices, its beauty and powers for rejuvenation. He takes us from the boys scuffling in the street—the "guilt and restlessness and muffled fate"—to "the vague influence of the distant stars" and tells us we then must siphon the whole smoky storm, like an Aladdin's lamp in reverse, "into a handful of inwardness." The world is inside us while we are in the world. (And vice versa: We are in the world because the world is inside us.)

I don't believe Rilke is arguing here for pure art. If anything, he is saying that self-containment—true self-containment— also contains Walt Whitman's multitudes. The poet's task, if we were to take Rilke's poem as credo, is to show us the handful of inwardness in each and every instance of outward worldly activity—even in "the changing and flying and fleeing of the clouds."

Yet the poem does not end on inwardness. The last line gives us another twist in the relationship between inside and outside: the outside world has been transformed into "a hand-ful of inwardness" that "now lies carefree in these open roses." The precious revelation—the interior connection—is both a bird in the hand and two birds in the bush: open the hand and the bird flies, keep it closed, and no one can know it is there. And the revelation must seem effortless—"carefree"—embed-ded in the icons of the physical world, yet buoyed by the in-tegrity of physical presence. Indeed, the poem itself unfolds like roses in a bowl, representing everything and yet "containing nothing but itself"; like them, it refuses to stay in one place, even as it unabashedly persists in being about nothing but it-self—i.e., an ever-expanding state of contemplation, the apo-theosis of reverie.

What do we contemplate nowadays? A couple of years ago a cable television station in Columbia, South Carolina, decided to fill empty air time by training a camera on an aquarium of trop-ical fish; jazz played in the background. When they eventually managed to slot a program during that time—which was late at night—viewers were so upset that they phoned the station in droves, complaining so fervently that the station was forced to reinstate the aquarium show!

What does this tell us about ourselves? That we're bored with conventional television programming, perhaps; that we like fish, perhaps—but isn't it the invitation to contemplation that the aquarium phenomenon offers? The erratic movements of the tropical fish remind us of the convoluted workings of our thoughts, the beautiful ramblings of our memories, sensory im-pressions and cognitive impulses. The fish, validated by the television screen, give us leave to daydream. With the advent of television, our contemplative gaze, rather than being directed both outward and inward simultaneously (as in Rilke's poem), has become directed entirely inward—so that, snared in our own mood shifts or the meta-reality of C-Span, Court TV, or the sit-com, we're oblivious to our true surroundings . . . oblivious, really, to ourselves.

In her landmark 1949 book, *The Life of Poetry*, Muriel Rukeyser says:

> Writing is only another way of giving—a courtesy, if you will, and a form of love.
>
> But does one write in order to give?
>
> One writes in order to feel: that is the fundamental mover.
>
> The more clearly one writes, the more clearly willboth the writer and the reader feel. But there must beimaginative truth—truth which is the health and strength and richness of imagination before poet or reader can approach the poem.

I think what Rukeyser means by "imaginative truth" is nothing else but a healthy interior life, as defined by an ability to connect to our inarticulate emotions and a willingness to admit that there are feelings that go beyond the catch-phrases of civilized discourse. Only then can we enter fully into the world of the imagination; only then can we, as Blake says in his poem "Auguries of Innocence":

> . . . see a World in a Grain of Sand,
> And a Heaven in a Wild Flower,
> Hold Infinity in the palm of your hand,
> And Eternity in an hour.

But what if our imaginations are as the poet H.D. described them in *Notes on Thought and Vision*?

Our minds, all of our minds, are like dull little houses, built more or less alike—a dull little city with rows of little detached villas, and here and there a more pretentious house, set apart from the rest, but in essentials, seen from a distance, one with the rest, all drab, all grey.

Each comfortable little home shelters a comfortable little soul—and a wall at the back shuts out completely any communication with the world beyond.

Man's chief concern is keeping his little house warm and making his little wall strong.

Outside is a great vineyard and grapes and rioting and madness and angers.

It is very dangerous.

Today, in our comfortable houses, the window of choice appears to be television. It's a small window, and we peer through it into smaller houses, smaller rooms, the shoebox theater's improbable world. And what do we see inside that flickering funhouse mirror? Family comedies, horror flicks, game shows, and chatter by the Famous for Fifteen Minutes crowd. Rather than bring the world into our living rooms, our TV news programs, sweetened by human interest stories and backup music, actually make us feel safe: instead of a global village we see a world composed of fiefdoms; inside the walls of our castle we know every person's comings and goings (soap opera and situation comedies provide accepted norms), and distant news give us the comforting sensation that the enemy is just outside someone else's gates . . . so let's sit back and soak up all the juicy details. Listen to the concluding stanzas of "Watching Television," a poem by Laurie Sheck:

At night it is so quiet;
the world hovers mute outside my window,

a face whose mouth is bandaged over,
a face I can neither touch nor send away.

But the gray faces on the screen still speak and speak;
they are faithful, they remain.
They glide like clouds through their gray air.
The red pulse of the columbine does not touch them.
Nor the ticking of the clock. Nor the cry of a child.

(from Io at Night)

~

For years the following scene would play daily at our house: Home from school, my daughter would heave her backpack off her shoulder and let it thud to the hall floor, then dump her jacket on top of the pile. My husband would tell her to pick it up—as he did every day—and hang it in the closet. Begrudgingly, with a snort and a hrrumph, she would comply. The ritual interrogation began:

"Hi, Aviva. How was school?"

"Fine."

"What did you do today?"

"Nothing."

And so it went, every day. We cajoled, we pleaded, we threatened with rationed ice cream sandwiches and new healthy vegetable casseroles, we attempted subterfuges such as: "What was Ms. Boyers wearing today?" or: "Any new pets in science class?" but her answer remained the same: I dunno.

Asked, however, about that week's episodes of "MathNet," her favorite series on Public Television's "Square One," or asked for a quick gloss of a segment of "Lois and Clark" that we happened to miss, and she'd spew out the details of a complicated story, complete with character development, gestures, every twist and back-flip of the plot.

Is TV greater than reality? Are we to take as damning evidence the soap opera stars attacked in public by viewers who obstinately believe in the on-screen villainy of Erica or Jeannie's evil twin? Is an estrangement from real life the catalyst behind the escalating violence in our schools, where children imitate the gun-'em-down pyrotechnics of cop-and-robber shows?

Such a conclusion is too easy. Yes, the influence of public media on our perceptions is enormous, but the relationship of projected reality—i.e., TV—to imagined reality—i.e., an existential moment—is much more complex. It is not that we confuse TV with reality, but that we prefer it to reality—the manageable struggle resolved in twenty-six minutes, the witty repartee within the family circle instead of the grunts and silence common to most real families; the sharpened conflict and defined despair instead of vague anxiety and invisible enemies. "Life, my friends, is boring. We must not say so," wrote John Berryman, and many years and "Dream Songs" later he leapt from a bridge in Minneapolis. But there is a devastating corollary to that statement: Life, friends, is ragged. Loose ends are the rule.

What happens when my daughter tells the television's story better than her own is simply this: the TV offers an easier tale to tell. The salient points are there for the plucking—indeed, they're the only points presented—and all she has to do is to recall them. Instant Nostalgia! Life, on the other hand, slithers about and runs down blind alleys and sometimes just fizzles at the climax. "The world is ugly, / And the people are sad," sings the country bumpkin in Wallace Stevens's "Gubinnal." Who isn't tempted to ignore the inexorable fact of our insignificance on a dying planet? We all yearn for our private patch of blue.

⁓

When I was growing up, there were two iron-clad rules at mealtime: No reading at the dinner table, and each person had to say one thing about their day before the meal was over. We usually proceeded clockwise, starting at my father's left hand with my brother, then me, my mom, my two younger sisters and, finally, my father. I dreaded dredging up some interesting anecdote from school or orchestra practice and struggled to strike the right balance—to hit upon an event that would be interesting enough to get me off the hook without being forced to elaborate. ("Is that all that happened to you today?" my father would exclaim. "Well, I feel sorry for you. What else?") I usually lost the struggle, but finally it became clear to me that the bout was rigged: The more I tried to avoid telling the story, the more questions I would be asked. In time, I realized that I enjoyed hearing from everyone else, which meant that they must have enjoyed hearing what I had to say, no matter how mundane I thought it sounded. I began to select the choicest details from the morass of a day's instructions, shaping it in my mind for the most succinct and entertaining delivery. Today I know that I was learning how to shape life—or, more precisely, memory. It gave me a handle on the day, a way of perceiving and grappling with my own flux.

This is the art form we are losing. We lost a chunk of it when we stopped writing letters, we lost a hunk when we poured our reveries into the prefabricated situations of television life. In time, real life slips away from us, too complicated and unnamable, and we turn with relief to a world that has been ordered for us. Whenever we have an opportunity for serious contemplation, we dull it with alcohol or sports or skitter around the edges, picking at the moment as nervously as a cat paws the fringe on a shawl. We deliberately choose the small and manageable moments so that we can fondle them, interpret them to death.

It often seems to me that where our capacity for inwardness has failed—or rather, where we have failed ourselves—film has stepped in. The best of cinema explores the relationship between the concrete world—i.e., what the camera sees—and the interior world, or consciousness—how the camera chooses to see. Intimacy can be established without a word—in the minute and sensuous sweep of the camera's eye over the lush grasses outside the ancestral home at the beginning of *Howard's End*, for example, or through a trick of the lens, as in Bertolucci's *Once Upon a Time in America*, when the mobster leader played by Robert De Niro, after brutally murdering a rival gangster, hides out from the Feds in an opium den, and the camera lens imitates his state of mind by gradually blurring as he smokes himself into oblivion.

But can film really give utterance to the ineffable urgings inside us? Attempts at decoding thought, at "showing" the workings of the mind, have been a consistent problem in the dramatic arts; talk, after all, is one of the primary vehicles of plot advancement, and there are only so many close-ups of Liv Ullmann's face—a face more expressive than most—tolerable in a full-length movie.

One of the most successful cinematic explorations of inwardness, Wim Wenders's 1987 film *Der Himmel über Berlin*— literally "The Sky, or Heaven, above Berlin," but released in this country under the oddly romantic title *Wings of Desire*—takes the other extreme: Words—not images caught by the camera's eye—are used to establish inwardness. I think it's significant that the script was a collaboration between rhapsodic filmmaker Wenders and the Austrian poet Peter Handke. The protagonists are two angels, Cassiel and Damiel, whose assigned "beat" is Berlin. As we discover, angels (and there are many of them, but Wenders is concentrating on Cassiel and Damiel) are invisible to human beings, although occasionally those more apt to blur distinctions between reality and imagination—children, the mentally handicapped—are aware of the angels' calming presence. The angels' only power is to witness the inner human life and, through a barely perceptible touch, console us when we are in extremity. Wenders takes the phrase "brushed by an angel's wing" literally; Cassiel and Damiel give courage to the despairing with a breath on the neck, a fingertip drawn lightly along a shoulder's curve.

But how are we mere mortals in the audience made privy to their witnessing? Through words. Whenever an angel draws near a human being, that person's thoughts become audible. We're slow to realize this at the movie's beginning: First we see the sky over Berlin, with clouds, then a shot of the angel Damiel, wings protruding from a wool overcoat, looking down from a building ledge. What we hear, though, as the camera swings to gaze at the street scene below, is a murmur of voices; nothing is comprehensible at first, and then, gradually, individual voices emerge from the babble. A woman bicycles by, and as she pedals, her thoughts spin into us: *Finally crazy, finally resolve. Finally crazy, finally quiet. Finally a fool, finally an inner light.* From the crammed interior of a car comes the driver's voice, in Turkish; we are not given a translation. Thoughts are picked up midstream and fade away as the angel moves through a crowd. Gradually our resistance dissolves, and we are at home with our consciousness, our interior selves. Contrary to dramatic tradition, where dialogue is the norm and the soliloquy or dramatic aside (in cinema, the voice-over) intrudes, in this film whenever actual spoken dialogue occurs, it is intrusive. And then comes a scene, stunningly rendered by Wenders, that's been the despair of many a novelist, poet, or director: the moment of death.

Damiel comes across a motorcycle accident. The young man, who has been thrown against the curb, is bleeding to death as bystanders look on helplessly. Through Damiel we "hear" the motorcyclist's thoughts, overlapping snatches of phrases ranging from exclamations of outrage—"What are you gawking at? Haven't you seen someone croak before?"—to shame—"Here, lying in a puddle!"—to remorse—"Karin, I should have told you yesterday . . . ." As his thoughts threaten to disintegrate into babbling fear, the angel takes the young man's head in his hands and helps him call out to the world he is leaving:

The spots from the first drops of rain.
The sun.
Bread and wine.
To skip.
Easter dinner.
The veins of the leaves.
The swaying grass.
The colors of stones.
Gravel at the bottom of the brook.
The white tablecloth at the picnic.
The dream of a house . . .
               . . . in the house.
The sleeper in the next room.
Quiet on Sunday.

This litany—no less than an invocation to the physical world—helps ease a dying man's agony. It reminds me of another litany, this one written shortly after the end of World War II—that point in history which Theodor Adorno called "Ground zero." Adorno posed the question: "After Auschwitz, is poetry possible?" The following poem was Günter Eich's chilling answer:

INVENTUR	INVENTORY
Dies ist meine Mütze,	This is my cap,
dies ist mein Mantel,	this is my coat,
hier mein Rasierzeug	here my shaving things
im Beutel aus Leinen.	in a pouch of linen.
Konservenbüchse:	Tin can:
Mein Teller, mein Becher:	my plate, my cup:

ich hab in das Weißblech	in the tin dish
den Namen geritzt.	I've scratched my name.
Geritzt hier mit diesem	Scratched here with this
kostbaren Nagel,	precious nail,
den vor begehrlichen	which I hide from
Augen ich berge.	jealous eyes.
Im Brotbeutel sind	In the bread bag is
ein Paar wollene Socken	a pair of wool socks
und einiges, was ich	and stuff I'll tell
niemand verrate,	no one about—
so dient es als Kissen	it serves as a pillow
nachts meinem Kopf.	nights for my head.
Die Pappe hier liegt	This cardboard here lies
zwischen mir und der Erde.	between me and the earth.
Die Bleistiftmine	Most of all I love
lieb ich am meisten:	the lead in the pencil:
Tags schreibt sie mir Verse,	it writes poems by day
die nachts ich erdacht.	that I thought up at night.
Dies ist mein Notizbuch,	This is my notebook,
dies meine Zeltbahn,	this my ground sheet,
dies ist mein Handtuch,	this is my hand towel,
dies ist mein Zwirn.	this is my twine.

In one instance a cornucopia of words; in the other, an impoverishment. Wim Wenders generates a state of inwardness through excess—words tumbling, words overlapping, underscoring and even obliterating each other until what we are listening to is the murmuring of consciousness, a symphony of human sighs that only in death will trickle to its conclusion. However, a lyric such as Günter Eich's poem (and in spite of its stark syntax and diminished vocabulary—or because of this—"Inventory" is a lyric poem) uses words sparingly, like stepping stones across a river, so that we can better hear the silence, the unworded depths, we traverse.

How can we, as poets in today's instantly over-communicative, informationally medicated society, extend that handful of inwardness? Not by flinging or dangling it as if to taunt others for their lack of sensitivity, not by tossing it at the public and running—but by daring, in the wilderness of our own progress, daring to speak heart-to-heart to the stranger? One way is to create a poetic space for the spirit to dream in, a world on a page which, through its smells and sounds and discriminating eye, entices us to enter it.

"Things that divine us we never touch." So begins Charles Wright's poem "The Southern Cross." He then beguiles us with a tantalizing string of phenomena that are there and not there, simultaneously:

> The black sounds of the night music,
> The Southern Cross, like the kite at the end of its string,
>
> And now this sunrise, and empty sleeve of a day,
> The rain just starting to fall, and then not fall,
>
> No trace of a story line.

As one of our most eloquent practitioners of the metaphysical, Charles Wright has perfected a lyric line rich with retractions and interruptions; rhetorical questions, sly tautologies, and rhapsodic non sequiturs are linked by commas, dashes, dropped lines, ellipses—all this in order to articulate the ineffable, to make inwardness palpable in the very knots and thumbholes of language. Here's a more recent example by Charles Wright, from his poem "December Journal":

The tongue cannot live up to the heart:
Raise the eyes of your affection to its affection
And let its equivalents
                    ripen in your body.
Love what you don't understand yet, and bring it to you.

From somewhere we never see comes everything that we do
          see.
What is important devolves
                    from the immanence of infinitude
In whatever our hands touch—
The other world is here, just under our fingertips.

From the simple, earthy diction of "The Southern Cross" to the philosophical vocabulary of "December Journal" is not so huge a leap as one might imagine. The shift from the graphic corporeality of the line "The tongue cannot live up to the heart" conceals a complex emotional topography; "Raise the eyes of your affection to its affection / And let its equivalents / ripen in your body" continues the game of "Now you touch it; now you don't," sketched in bolder strokes, in "The Southern Cross." The difference is that the poet is actually mounting and descending in the words themselves—using levels of language to set up a catacomb within the reader where the very sounds and shapes and histories of the words reverberate, mingling in a remarkably supple palimpsest through which the poem's meaning wells up, each layer building on and intertwining with the last.

"I write for myself and strangers. The strangers, dear Readers, are an afterthought." With this comment, Gertrude Stein located, I believe, the essential appointment of the writer. The artist cannot seek approval, though she may long for it. She dare not consider the reactions of friends or family; she must not remember such words as "policy" or "political correctness." Alone in her room, the circle of light on the page, alone with the exhilarating yet terrifying knowledge that each of us is less than a speck in the cosmic dust storm, she presumes to speak: first out of her great solitude, her "guilt and restlessness and muffled fate," then to another soul—this communication no more than a whisper, like Federico Garcia Lorca's "Deep Song," which "comes from the first sob and the first kiss." The poet presumes to speak, and the strangers are the ones who listen.

A great poem will contain these polarities; it will make us acutely aware of our individual heartbeat, even while it creates a community of whispers. Emily Dickinson wrote:

> The Soul selects her own Society —
> Then — shuts the Door —
> To her divine Majority —
> Present no more.

And Walt Whitman:

> Camerado, this is no book,
> Who touches this touches a man,
> (Is it night? Are we here together alone?)

What can we leave behind after our sojourn on this earth is over? Monuments? A rather stiff and silent legacy, though monuments, we tell ourselves, continue to live through the dreams they call forth. Legislation? Perhaps, if the legislation changes history, such as the Constitution and the Bill of Rights, or the landmark decision of *Brown v. the Board of Education.* Our children will carry traces of our features, even our characters and personalities, perhaps anecdotes—but what of our personal essence? What of our inwardness can we hope will last after we're gone?

This is where poetry enters—where innermost thoughts are

the rule rather than the embarrassing aberration, where what matters—more than power or position or automobile or designer label or grade point average—is simply our being in the world. And when we come to this recognition of ourselves, we can embrace it with relief or we can shrink from it as something perilous, something that would rob us of our sanity. Of course, if sanity means to be ever efficient, to follow the dictates of public opinion (that hydra-headed monster); if to be sane means to squelch any niggling doubt or fear or joy that might interfere with the daily operation of our lifestyle, then yes, poetry is dangerous, as any artistic communication is dangerous. Then the messenger runs the grave risk of being killed: We deny funds for the arts because they are "non-utilitarian," we blacklist movie directors under charges of un-American activities, we condemn performance artists for "obscenity."

The poet H.D. would agree: Outside the dull little houses of our minds, she wrote, "is a great vineyard and grapes and rioting and madness and angers. It is very dangerous." Yes—but outside is also where the grapes are.

⁓

If, as Bachelard claims, "Poetry is one of the destinies of speech," then what happened to me in that old house in France this past summer was a coming full circle to the origins of man's essential distinction from the beasts: wonder, and the desire to communicate that wonder. I retreated from the window of the world in order to find another way to speak to you, to find a private vocabulary for a public purpose. Poetic language dreams. And there occurs, in the ideal creative state, a balance between inner and outer worlds, self-containing yet transformative—not a fistful, not a pinch, but a measured handful of inwardness. Yes, it is terrifying to walk out into the arena, under the roar of the bloodthirsty, wine-soaked spectators, with just a hand held out—but someone will reach out to take it.

references

Atwood, Margaret. 1987. Interview in *Ms.* Magazine. January.

Bachelard, Gaston. 1971. *The Poetics of Reverie*, translated by Daniel Russell. Boston: Beacon Press.

Bachelard, Gaston. 1994. *The Poetics of Space*, translated by Maria Jolas. Boston: Beacon Press. Copyright © 1964 Orion Press, New York, N.Y.; copyright © 1969 Beacon Press.

Berryman, John. 1969. "Dream Song No. 46." From *The Dream Songs*. New York: Farrar, Straus and Giroux. Copyright © 1969 by John Berryman.

Blake, William. 1991. "Auguries of Innocence." From *Songs of Innocence and of Experience*. Princeton: Princeton University Press. Copyright ©1991 The Tate Gallery and the William Blake Trust.

Brooks, Gwendolyn. 1987. "A Song in the Front Yard." From *A Street in Bronzeville*. Reprinted in *Blacks*. Chicago: David Company. Copyright © 1987 by The David Company.

Dickinson, Emily. 1991. "The Soul Selects Her Own Society." From *Emily Dickinson: Collected Poems*. Philadelphia: Running Press Book Publishers. Copyright © 1991 by Running Press Book Publishers.

Dove, Rita. 1980. "Adolescence—III," "Geometry," "Five Elephants." From *The Yellow House on the Corner*. Pittsburgh: Carnegie-Mellon University Press. Copyright © 1980 by Rita Dove.

Dove, Rita. 1983. "A Father Out Walking on the Lawn," "Fiametta Breaks Her Peace." From *Museum*. Pittsburgh: Carnegie-Mellon University Press. Copyright © 1983 by Rita Dove.

Dove, Rita. 1986. "Sunday Greens." From *Thomas and Beulah*. Pittsburgh: Carnegie-Mellon University Press. Copyright © 1986 by Rita Dove.

Dove, Rita. 1991. "The House That Jill Built." From *The Writer on Her Work*, vol. 2, edited by Janet Sternberg. New York: W. W. Norton & Co.

Eich, Günter. 1960. "Inventur." From *Ausgewählte Gedichte*, edited by Walter Höllerer. Translated by Rita Dove.

H.D. (Hilda Doolittle). 1982. Excerpt from *Notes on Thought and Vision and The Wise Sappho*. San Francisco: City Lights Books. Copyright © 1982 by the Estate of Hilda Doolittle.

Hughes, Langston. 1994. "I, too." From *The Collected Poems of Langston Hughes*. New York: Knopf; distributed by Random House.

Hughes, Langston. 1941. "Song to a Negro Wash-woman." From *Gold-

en Slippers, edited by Arna Bontemps. New York: Harper & Row. Copyright © 1941 and renewed by Langston Hughes. Reprinted by permission of Harold Ober Associates, Inc.

Lee, Li-Young. 1990. "This Room and Everything in It." From *The City in Which I Love You*. Brockport, N.Y.: BOA Editions, Limited. Copyright © 1990 by Li-Young Lee.

Levine, Philip. 1979. "Starlight." From *Ashes: Poems New & Old*. New York: Atheneum. Copyright © 1979 by Philip Levine.

Levine, Philip. 1985. "The House." From *Sweet Will*. New York: Atheneum. Copyright © 1985 by Philip Levine.

Merwin, W. S. 1988. "The Horizons of Rooms." From *The Rain in the Trees*. New York: Alfred A. Knopf; distributed by Random House. Copyright © 1988 by W. S. Merwin.

Orr, Gregory. 1973. "The Room." From *Burning the Empty Nests*. New York: Harper & Row. Copyright © 1973 by Gregory Orr.

Rich, Adrienne. 1975. "A Valediction Forbidding Mourning." From *Poems: Selected & New, 1950-1974*. New York: W.W. Norton, Inc. Copyright © 1975 by W. W. Norton, Inc.

Rilke, Rainer Maria. 1984. "A Bowl of Roses." From *New Poems (1907)*, translated by Edward Snow. San Francisco: North Point Press. Translations copyright © 1984 by Edward Snow.

Rukeyser, Muriel. 1948. "Then I Saw What the Calling Was." From *The Green Wave*. New York: Doubleday & Company, Inc. Copyright © 1948 by Muriel Rukeyser.

Rukeyser, Muriel. 1949. Excerpt from *The Life of Poetry*. New York: Current Books.

Sexton, Anne. 1981. "Locked Doors." From *The Complete Poems*. Boston: Houghton Mifflin. Copyright © 1981 by Linda Gray Sexton and Loring Conant, Jr.

Sheck, Laurie. 1990. "Watching Television." From *Io at Night*. New York: Alfred A. Knopf, Inc.; distributed by Random House. Copyright ©1990 by Laurie Sheck.

Tolson, Melvin B. 1965. *Harlem Gallery*. New York: Twayne Publishers, Inc. Copyright © 1965 by Twayne Publishers, Inc.

Tuéni, Nadia. 1992. "Nothing But a Man" translated by Willis Barnstone. From *Women Poets from Antiquity to Now*, edited by Aliki and Willis Barnstone. New York: Schocken Books.

Whitman, Walt. 1968. "So Long!" (1860). From *A Choice of Whitman's Verse,* edited by Donald Hall. London: Faber & Faber.

Wright, Charles. 1981. "The Southern Cross." From *The Southern Cross*. New York: Random House. Copyright ©1981 by Charles Wright.

Wright, Charles. 1990. "December Journal." From *The World of the Ten Thousand Things: Poems 1980-1990*. New York: Farrar, Straus & Giroux. Copyright © 1990 by Charles Wright

Rita Dove. Photo by Fred Viebahn.

autobiography

Rita Dove, Poet Laureate Consultant in Poetry, at a press conference at the Library of Congress, October 1993. Photo by Jim Higgins.

Even in the crib, it seems, I was a night person. "I remember waking up at three in the morning," my mother is fond of saying, "because I heard some noises coming from the nursery. And when I tiptoed in, terrified that a burglar had slipped into my baby's room, what did I find?"—here she pauses for effect—"Just little old you, playing contentedly in the pitch dark!" According to family legend, my parents tried everything to put me on "normal" time: eliminating naps during the day, keeping me up past midnight, submitting me to a sequence of aerobic exercises in an effort to tire me out. Nothing worked. To this day I remain more mentally alert in the hours between midnight and 5 A.M.

I would like to believe that I became a poet because of this unusual body clock, but I'm afraid I didn't entertain notions of becoming a writer until well into my undergraduate college years. Not that I didn't indulge in all of the pastimes commonly associated with the literary mind; from the age of six I loved to read, and by seven or eight I had begun writing my own stories and poems.

I made two "breakthroughs" as a child writer: one in prose, and one in poetry. During a free-choice period in fourth grade, I wrote an Easter poem called "The Rabbit with the Droopy Ear." Once I had the title, I began writing with no idea whatsoever of how the rabbit was going to be cured of his physical defect:

Mr. Rabbit was big and brown,
But he always wore a frown.
He was sad, even though Spring was here,
Because he had one droopy ear.

They were the handsomest ears in town;
'Cept one went up, and one hung down.
And to think Easter was almost here!
Alas for the rabbit with the droopy ear.

But I kept writing, deeper and deeper into the narrative, and by the penultimate stanza, the solution "occurred" with no apparent effort of my own:

The Rabbit went to wise old owl,
And told his tale 'twixt whine and howl.
The owl just leaned closer to hear
And said, "I know the cure for your droopy ear."

The next day everyone gathered 'round to see
The incident at the old oak tree.
Mr. Rabbit hung upside down
From a branch on the tree, and gone was his frown.

Hip, hip hooray — let's toast him a cup,
For now both ears were hanging *up!*
All the animals raised a cheer:
Hooray for the rabbit with the two *straight* ears!

It was as if the poem itself, through its cadences and narrative thrust, had told *me* the answer.

"Chaos," my first attempt at extended prose, was written over the period of one semester, also in fourth grade. Each Monday afternoon the teacher would allot twenty-five minutes for spelling; after going over the new spelling list, we were supposed to do the exercises in our text. I would quickly finish them (usually something like, "Use each spelling word in a sentence"), and then I'd write the next chapter of my epic science-fiction saga. The only rules I set for myself were: (1) each spelling word had to be used in the tense/conjugation presented, (2) the order of the list must be honored, and (3) no peeking at next week's list. Needless to say, I had no idea what developments in plot or character were going to occur. Again, it was the language itself that led me on; I was open to the adventure.

Though I obviously relished creating my own stories and poems, at that age it never occurred to me to think about writing as more than a pastime. I had no idea that one could grow up and become a writer, much less how to develop a life around writing.

I spent my childhood and youth in Akron, Ohio, as a first generation middle-class black child. Both sets of grandparents were blue-collar workers who had moved Up North as part of the Great Migration of rural southern blacks to the northern urban centers during the 1910s and '20s. My parents were the first in their working-class families to achieve advanced degrees. My mother graduated from high school at the age of sixteen with a full scholarship to Howard University but her parents decided their daughter was too young to be sent into the wide world, so she attended the local secretarial school. My father earned a master's degree in chemistry from the University of Akron. (He also completed all the course work toward the doctorate, but could not afford to take the time off from his menial job in order to write his dissertation.)

I and my three siblings (two younger sisters, one older brother) came of age in a supportive but strict environment. We knew we were expected to carry "the prize"—the respect that had been earned—a little further along the line. We had to do our best at all times; there were no excuses.

Of course we were aware of discrimination, but not as

something that affected us directly—although our father had been a direct victim of prejudice in my lifetime. After graduating with honors, he applied for a job as an analytical chemist at the Goodyear Tire and Rubber Company, the chief employer in Akron. Unlike his white schoolmates, some of whom he had tutored in organic chemistry, my father was passed over for a chemist's post (despite graduating at the top of his class) and instead was offered the position of elevator operator. With a wife, son, and another child (me) on the way, he could ill afford to be indignant; he accepted the menial job and for years ferried his former classmates from floor to floor. Finally, consistent protest against this racist foolishness by one of his former professors and a change in Goodyear's management ended this indignity, and my father became the first black chemist (he's retired now) in the rubber industry.

I was not aware of any of this. My parents raised us to be proud of our heritage, and cautioned us against the subtle reach of prejudice; but they were careful not to dash our hopes too early: Though they related historical indignities and racist incidents, they also conveyed the impression that times were changing, and our abilities would be recognized.

Education was the key: That much we knew, and so I was a good student. I brought home straight A's on my report card and hoarded the shiny dimes I got for each of them. Which is not to say I didn't like school—I adored learning new things and looked forward to what intellectual adventures each school day would bring; some of the luckiest magic in the world was to open a book and come away from it wiser after having been lost in its pages.

≈

Among my earliest influences were relatives who loved to tell good stories; some forms of popular entertainment—rock and roll lyrics, action comic books, *MAD* magazine—had an impact on me as well. I was not reading "pulp literature" exclusively; I devoured all kinds of writing. But it was pulp literature that, as a child, I sought to imitate by creating my own—perhaps I felt that I had a better chance of emulating formulaic writing rather than Shakespeare's sonnets (which I began reading around the age of twelve) or James Baldwin's *The Fire Next Time*.

From the time I was eight until I turned fourteen, a typical summer would run something like this: My brother, who is two years my senior, would declare himself the editor-in-chief of our summer vacation neighborhood newspaper; after lengthy negotiations, I would finally attain the status of feature editor. (All of this, of course, took place before we actually set down a single word.) Invariably, I would quit in protest against his autocratic directives and establish my own magazine, called *Poet's Delight;* however, if I remember correctly, I never completed an issue of that either. (I usually managed to write one poem about autumn so that I could color in a cover design featuring a large maple tree and a rather dreamy person lying under its boughs.) But I put far more energies into my comic book heroines, who were modeled after the standard heroes of the day: Jet Girl (with her dog, Jet Zoommano), Remarkable Girl (with her dog, Remarkark), Space Girl, and Lightning Bolt, a female variation on Flash Gordon and the Human Torch. My brother and I also composed many an R & B song and recorded them using the impressive sea-green microphone that my father had hooked up to the stereo. And we produced radio plays for the delight and edification of any adults we could corral into sitting through them. These audio dramas always included a raging waterfall and a lightning storm, both of which we gleefully created over the kitchen sink.

I read everything my brother was reading. He was into science fiction, so I'd read his *Analog* and *Fantasy and Science Fiction* magazines after he was finished with them. One science fiction story fascinated me in particular: a retarded boy builds a sculpture from discarded materials—coke bottles, scrap iron, string, bottle caps. The town looks on, amused. Then one day, the boy disappears. The narrator of the story, investigating the mystery, finds that the "sculpture" is actually a machine that activates a doorway into another dimension; he steps through into this alternate universe, which is the mirror image of his town, and when he makes his way to the town square he discovers a statue erected to—who else?—the village idiot.

I loved this story—the idea that the dreamy, mild, scatterbrained boy of one world could be the hero in another. In a way, I identified with that village idiot, because the place I felt most alive was between the pages of a book, while in real life I was painfully shy and awkward.

What I remember most about rainy summer days is browsing the bookshelves in our solarium to see if there were any new additions. I grew up with those rows of books; I knew where every book was shelved and immediately spotted newcomers. And after months had gone by without new acquisitions, I would tell myself: Okay, I guess I'll try this one—and then discover that the very book I had been avoiding because of a drab cover or small print was actually a wonderful read. Louis Untermeyer's *Treasury of Best Loved Poems,* for example, had a sickeningly sweet lilac and gold cover and was forbiddingly thick, but I finally pulled it off the shelf and discovered a cornucopia of emotional and linguistic delights, from "The Ballad of Barbara Fritchie," which I adored for its sheer length and rather numbing rhymes, to Langston Hughes's dazzlingly syncopated "Dream Boogie."

There was also Shakespeare—daunting for many years because it was the complete oeuvre, in matching wine-red volumes so thick they looked more like over-sized bouillon cubes than books . . . and yet it was that ponderous title *The Complete Works of William Shakespeare* that enticed me, because here was a lifetime's work—a lifetime!—in two compact, dense packages. I began with the long poem "The Rape of Lucrece" (looking for the rape, of course, which I couldn't locate); then I stumbled onto a few sonnets, which I found beautiful but too adult in theme, and finally wandered into the plays—first *Romeo and Juliet,* then *Macbeth, Julius Caesar, A Midsummer Night's Dream, Twelfth Night.*

I was enthralled by the power of Shakespeare's language, and especially by my discovery that poetry was spinning the story. Of course I did not understand every single word, but I was too young to know that this was supposed to be difficult; besides, no one was waiting to test me on aspects of structure and content, and so, free from pressure, I dove in.

Although I loved books, I had no aspirations to be a *writer.* I liked to *write*—all those books had made me into a demanding reader, and sometimes, on long summer days when I ran out of material to read, or my legs had fallen asleep because I had been curled up on the couch for hours on end, I invented my own stories.

Most were never finished. Those that were, I didn't show to anyone. I didn't think making up stories was something ordinary people admitted to doing. There were no living role models for me—a writer was a dead white male, usually with a long white beard to match.

Finally, in twelfth grade, I had a crucial experience. My English teacher, Miss Oechsner, took me to a book signing in a downtown hotel. She didn't ask me if I'd like to go—she got my parents' permission instead, signed me and another guy out of school one day (that other guy is a literature professor at Berkeley now, by the way) and took us to meet a REAL LIVE AUTHOR. He was John Ciardi, a poet who had translated Dante's *Divine Comedy,* which I had heard of, vaguely. That day I realized that writers were real people, and that it was possible to be a writer, to write down a poem or story in the intimate sphere of one's own room, and then share it with the world.

That same year, 1970, I was chosen as a Presidential Scholar, one of a hundred-odd high school seniors nationwide invited to Washington, D.C., to receive a medal. The telegram came on a school night in May, a little after dinner. "Western Union for you, Rita," Dad hollered. This bit of news made no sense at all, but I came to the door to sign for the first telegram in my life, tore open the envelope, and unfolded the dingy yellow page:

AS 1970 PRESIDENTIAL SCHOLAR, YOU ARE AMONG THE OUTSTANDING HIGH SCHOOL SENIORS IN OUR COUNTRY. I SEND YOU MY WARM CONGRATULATIONS ON THIS WELL-EARNED DISTINCTION, AND INVITE YOU TO MEET ME AT THE WHITE HOUSE ON JUNE FOURTH. COMPLETE DETAILS FOLLOW.

RICHARD NIXON

What was this, a joke? But my parents were solemnly considering this piece of sorcery as if it might mean something. They phoned Miss Oechsner who, it turned out, had recommended me in the first place. And so, a few weeks later, I took the first plane ride in my life, a forty-minute hop to National Airport. I made it all the way to Georgetown University before throwing up in a wastebasket in the lobby where all the Presidential Scholars had been gathered.

Oddly enough, I don't remember much about those three days in Washington. I think I was too nervous, or it was simply too much: We toured the monuments, attended lectures and panel discussions arranged for our benefit, and prepared for the medal ceremony at the White House. When word got out that our group was planning to hand the president a petition protesting the Vietnam War, Nixon's aide H. R. Haldeman admonished us as if we were nasty children, and not the crème de la crème of American Youth, and the president opted just to deliver a speech without shaking each of our hands as originally planned.

Still, the pomp and circumstance was substantial for a bunch of eighteen-year-old-kids, two from each state in the Union.

The "Personality Questionnaire" I had to fill out for the Presidential Scholar press packet included that popular section called "self-description," with this directive: "Which three adjectives would you use to describe your personality?" Two of my three attributes were "dreamy" and "mild." Nevertheless, when I entered Miami University (in Oxford, Ohio) in the fall of 1970, I listed my major as "pre-law," because that was what was expected of me. No one, and especially not my parents, had said this explicitly. But most of the adults I knew would make chance comments on the behavior and goals of television characters and neighbors, and so were sublimely involved in planning my life. Earlier, I had leafed through *Ebony* and *Jet* magazines, dreaming of the days when I would reap the rewards of my efforts in school by becoming a doctor's or lawyer's wife; now I had a generalized, blandly motivated ambition to become the doctor or lawyer myself. Wasn't it the obligation of a straight-A student to become such an authority figure on the top rungs of the ladder of community recognition and social reputation? And so I matriculated at Miami University convinced that pre-law was the appropriate— indeed, the only—career for someone like me. I had neglected one tiny detail, however: I had never shown an interest in the practical workings of the judicial system.

Needless to say, I changed my major four times before hitting my sophomore year—from pre-law to psychology, then German and, finally, English—until I could figure out what I wanted to do.

Fate struck again. Having placed out of freshman English, I enrolled in advanced composition to fulfill part of my core curriculum requirement. Six weeks into the semester, the professor was hospitalized, and the creative writing instructor took over. Milton White strode into class, his snowy white hair dipping dramatically over a tanned brow, horn-rimmed glasses contrasting with his cobalt blue Italian suit. "We're going to tell stories!" he announced, and spent the rest of the time going from person to person, asking for the opening lines of a "story." Terrified but strangely energized, we scrambled to think up racy plots; when my turn came I stalled for time by spinning out a description of the scene: "It's chilly this afternoon," I began, but before I could think further, Professor White interrupted. "Wait!" he shouted. "Did you notice how you began?" I hesitated, terrified. "You started out in the present tense," he said, "and captured the reader's attention; he's in the moment immediately. That's what you want to do. Whaddya know—you've got talent!" He spun around to confront the next student, but I heard no more; I was hooked.

In the fall of my junior year, I had to admit to myself that I had been arranging my course schedule around available creative writing classes. During the break in a poetry workshop, one of my classmates spoke woefully of an incident that summer when a friend of his family inquired what he planned to do with his English degree, and he had answered that he intended to become a professor. "Why didn't I say what I really want?" he exclaimed to a small group of us hanging around the vending machine. "Why didn't I just come out and say I want to be a poet?"

When I went home for Thanksgiving weekend, I first told my mother that I wanted to be a poet. "You better tell your father yourself," my mother replied; but all my father did was to swallow, lower his newspaper, and say: "Well, if that's what you want to do, all right. I've never really understood poetry, so please don't be upset if I don't read it." That was good enough for me; in fact, it was the best encouragement possible: an honest *bon voyage* as I set off on my adult career.

If I were to name extra-literary influences on my life and art, two come to mind immediately: music and German.

In fourth grade everyone in our class was given a Tonette, a black plastic wind instrument that bore a stubby resemblance to a recorder. Later that year, the music teacher asked those children demonstrating "musical aptitude" if we would like to learn a *real* instrument. My brother had gone through the same winnowing process two years earlier and now played the clarinet in the junior high band. Rejecting all wind and brass instruments, therefore, as a matter of course, I considered the array of strings. Everyone else chose violin, viola was a girl's name, the double bassist never got to play the melody. That left the violoncello. I was slightly taken aback by its size; I had expected something about the size of a guitar. But I had made my choice, so I stuck with it, and soon I grew to love the deep, haunting tones that poured from that wooden box whenever I bowed the strings properly. A year later I was recommended for private lessons once a week at the Akron Conservatory of Music, a renovated church with vaulted ceilings and delicious dark wood moldings; I was immediately entranced and decided that I would play cello forever just to be allowed to linger in those sun-stroked halls. I joined the Akron Youth Symphony and later, in high school, also did a few gigs as part of a jazz quintet (flute, keyboard, drums, cello, voice). I played with the Miami University orchestra and have studied music ever since.

The only time I was not actively involved in music was when the other extra-literary influence on my life and art began to take shape, during my Fulbright year in West Germany. After graduating from Miami University *summa cum laude* with a bachelor of arts degree in English (with creative writing emphasis) in December of 1973, I worked as a secretary with a contracting firm before flying to Europe in June of 1974. A smattering of other Fulbrighters were on the plane as well, and we had a grand and noisy time together. After negotiating my way through passport control and customs, I was feeling pretty cocky, striding through the Frankfurt airport, when I collided with another traveler. "*Entschuldigung*," he muttered, and went on his way. But I stood there, petrified, and suddenly heard it all around me: Everyone spoke *German*—everybody!—and they spoke rapidly, much more rapidly than I was accustomed to from German Conversation 202. How would I ever survive?

Two months of intensive language immersion (after four hours of class, I'd go back to my apartment and watch dubbed *Bonanza* episodes) at the Goethe Institute in Schwäbisch Hall, an idyllic river town in southern Germany, did the trick. I went on to study modern European literature at the University of Tübingen, where the noted author-critic Walter Jens held a chair in the Department of German Language and Literature, and where, in the early nineteenth century, the poet Hölderlin had spent the long last years of his life "mad as a fox," jotting down wildly disjointed poems of haunting beauty in a yellow tower overlooking the Neckar River.

I spoke, breathed, even dreamed in German. Switching to English with other American students became increasingly difficult, translating for visiting Americans nigh to impossible. To survive in Germany required a certain degree of self-sufficiency: Laundry was hung outside even in the dead of winter, and when I went shopping, I had to bag my own groceries. My self-confidence was growing; I learned to speak up during discussions, since *interrupt or forever hold your peace* seemed to be the brutal rule. And for the first time I saw my country from another vantage point. Although I understood my German classmates' image of the United States as a land of technicolor riches and abominable poverty, exalted beliefs (*We hold these truths to be self-evident . . .*) and intransigent racism, I insisted on differentiation; we argued after class, over *Kaffee und Kuchen,* during impromptu get-togethers late at night. The more I pointed out the errors in their simplistic appraisals and repudiated generalizations, the more complicated, and open to doubt, everything I believed in became—democracy, equality, the basic goodness of humanity. When I insisted that not all black Americans live either in Harlem or the Deep South, I remembered what my American history textbooks had reported and what they had chosen to ignore. This fascination with the underside of history—its vanquished and oppressed peoples, its ordinary citizens and unsung heroes—has accompanied me ever since.

When I returned to the United States in the summer of 1975, I entered graduate school at the University of Iowa's Writer's Workshop. The competition was as fierce as I had been led to fear; but after a year of speaking German, the intellectual fencing and literary hobnobbing that went on at Iowa seemed pretty small potatoes. Our teachers were excellent, and most of my peers were kind, although some were overly anxious and others cunning. Since I was the only black member of the workshop, however, I was pretty much left out of the Royal Hunt for a Pecking Order: I believe my race made me less of a threat—since this fact, at least in the subconscious minds of my classmates, doomed me to be an outsider, never to be on equal footing with them. On the other hand, I was the only student in the workshop who appeared in that year's major publication, *The American Poetry Anthology*. (The editor, Daniel Halpern, had visited Miami University two summers before and accepted for his magazine, *Antaeus*, the same poems which he then reprinted in the anthology.)

In my second year at Iowa I met my husband-to-be, the German novelist Fred Viebahn. Fred came to Iowa as part of the International Writing Program, which brought established authors to the "heartland of America" every fall semester. Each of these writers was asked to deliver a two-hour lecture on a subject of their choice. Eager to maintain my fluency in German, I had volunteered to translate whatever texts the German guest writer might consider using to illustrate his lecture.

We met on Fred's first day in the country, September 1, 1976. In fact, he was ferried straight from the Des Moines airport to a party being held in honor of the international authors at program director Paul Engle's house; I had been invited as Fred's potential translator. When we met a week later to choose the sections from his novels to be translated, we discovered that we had similar working patterns.

"I usually write until four in the morning or so," I said.

"That's nothing," Fred replied. "I stay up till at least five or six."

"Good for you," was my response to this bit of machismo. That night he called me at four to see if I was truly up and alert, and we talked for over an hour. We repeated this practice for more than a week, getting to know each other through conversation in the wee hours of the night before retiring separately to our respective beds. Early on we mused about a coincidence that struck us both as providential: The title of Fred's first novel, published in 1969, was *Die Schwarzen Tauben,* the German translation of the English name the protagonists, a high school rock band in Cologne in the mid-sixties, had given themselves: *The Black Doves.*

After receiving my M.F.A. in the spring of 1977, I was in a quandary. During the winter I had interviewed at Florida State University; convinced I could not possibly live in Tallahassee, much less produce any poems there, I had turned down their offer of a tenure track assistant professor position, a decision my classmates declared insane. Fred, who had been writer-in-residence at the University of Texas at Austin for the spring semester, and I planned to return to his stomping grounds in West Berlin to live a free-lance life. (Prior to Iowa, Fred had made his living by writing for German radio, television, and newspapers.)

Fate intervened, however, in the form of a farewell party for another German writer who was completing his semester as writer-in-residence at Oberlin College, only an hour from Akron. After transporting all of my gear from Iowa to my parents' house, Fred drove to Oberlin to see his friend while I stayed at home to convince my parents that this indeed was the man I wanted to marry. Fred returned with the startling news that Oberlin College had offered him a visiting professorship in the German Department, replacing sabbatical leaves.

During our two years in Oberlin, Fred taught German literature and wrote and directed bilingual plays for the annual German theater course. I took classes in modern dance and silversmithing, sewed our wedding outfits, and completed most of the work on what would become my first book of poems, *The Yellow House on the Corner.* Fearful that "Iowa" was still looking over my shoulder, I began writing short stories in order to escape the trap of the "workshop poem." A bit of that apprenticeship prose was later refined and included in my collection *Fifth Sunday.*

When I discovered I could not, as a nonstudent, sign up for private cello lessons at the Conservatory, I switched to the bass viola da gamba, an early cousin to the cello whose plaintive, reedy sound is produced by a fretted fingerboard and six gut strings. This chance development had its repercussions in later life, sparking an interest in medieval and Renaissance music that has continued into the present. (In recent years I have played gamba with several consorts in North Carolina and Virginia. For my fortieth birthday in 1992, Fred surprised me with a bass viol, custom made by one of the two contemporary viol builders in North America: My gamba, a replica of a seventeenth-century English original, displays as its scrollpiece the hand-carved head of a black woman, modeled after Albrecht Dürer's 1521 sketch *The Negress Katharina.*) Through playing gamba I have acquired, over the years, a more intricate understanding of rhythmic variations, and through early music—which, in its irregular measures and constant modulations, resembles modern jazz—have fallen in love all over again with the pleasure of music. I am quite certain this music has spilled into my poems, which are modulated by shifting word patterns and syncopation through internal rhyme and enjambment.

~

The two years in Oberlin and the two years immediately following, spent mostly in Israel and Germany, were truly my "salad days"—I had few responsibilities and little money, although the windfall of a National Endowment for the Arts creative writing grant in 1978 allowed me a modicum of financial security. We put the money in the bank as our collateral against starvation.

At the end of our first spring in Oberlin, after Fred had accepted a second year as sabbatical replacement, we sat down to decide what we were going to do with the summer between. Our lease on the rental house was up; we would have to look for new lodgings the following fall. Nothing bound us for the summer to this town or, for that matter, to America.

Fred and I arrived by car ferry in Dublin, Ireland, at the beginning of June 1978. We had rented a house in Dun Laoghaire, just south of Dublin, purely on the recommendation of an acquaintance of an Irish playwright who had been in residence at Oberlin that spring, and now we drove into the appointed neighborhood with trepidation. To our relief, the house was airy and welcoming, with several large windows facing a neighborhood square and a narrow but sunny garden out back. The owners met us with a big smile and the confession they, too, were a mixed couple (Catholic and Protestant), gave us the keys, and left for their summer house on the west coast.

Fred had a September deadline for a novel with his publisher, so we spent the next three months writing, seeing very little of Ireland (except on a few day-trip dashes) but feeling its muses nonetheless. On a typical day we would rise at four in the afternoon, just in time to gulp down a cup of coffee and rush to the market before closing; each day we tried a different variety of fresh fish; if necessary, we would also refill our liter bottles from huge oak barrels of sherry. Often we would take a stroll along the pier, sometimes all the way to the Joyce Tower. (*Come up, Kinch. Come up, you fearful jesuit.*) Back home, we'd make dinner and talk and read and watch television until it went off the air at midnight; afterwards we would retire to our separate studies (Fred in the living room on the third floor and I in the ground floor dining room, peat fire at my back) and write until the milkman arrived at sunrise. I was working on a novel which—major revisions, a dozen years, and hundreds of discarded pages later—would begin to take on a resemblance to the manuscript that was to become *Through the Ivory Gate.* In between bursts of writing I would read *Ulysses,* alternating with sections of Richard Ellmann's biography of Joyce. Occasionally this routine was interrupted by a visit from a charming but mysterious Irish friend of our playwright acquaintance, who would pop up to take us on day trips to various places of interest along the eastern Irish coast, present us with tickets to Makem and Clancy or James Galway or a Brendan Behan play, and then would disappear just as mysteriously and swiftly.

By the end of August, Fred had finished his fourth novel, *Die Fesseln der Freiheit,* and I had written half of a novel and several poor poems (too much Yeats in the air!) which luckily have never seen the light of publication.

Our time in Oberlin ended in May of 1979. That summer Fred was invited as a guest of the city of Jerusalem to spend three-months at Mishkenot Sha'ananim, a scholars' and artists' colony ensconced in a former caravanserai facing Mount Zion. We revised our habits to rise at 11:00 A.M. to the whitewashed, light-filled arches and corridors of our two-story apartment and the amazing views of the Old City from our windows; it was like living in a Bible picture book. Often we set out to explore the nooks and crannies of the city in the dog hours of the afternoon, when the shadows of the labyrinthian medina provided some respite from the heat. As the evening sun threw a golden-pink shawl over King David's tower, we returned to our terrace overlooking the valley between the Old and the New City and read until dinner, then retreated to our desks to write until three or four in the morning. From Jerusalem I mailed the manuscript of *The Yellow House on the Corner* to several publishers in the United States; word of its acceptance by Carnegie-Mellon University Press came in November at the German Academy in Rome, where we made a brief stop to intercept our forwarded mail on our way from Israel to Germany.

With no sabbatical openings to fill and no job prospects on the horizon, we had decided to revert to our original plan from two years earlier—before fate sent us to Oberlin—to earn our living as free-lance writers in Germany. We sublet a sunless, one-room apartment in Wedding, a blue collar district of West Berlin; a huge tiled oven in one corner provided the heat, to which end we hauled two bags of charcoal briquettes up three flights of stairs every other winter day. I wrote at the desk in the main room while Fred took the small circular table in the kitchen alcove. When this proved too cramped, the girlfriend of an acquaintance offered her apartment, vacant during university vacations. The only catch was that there was no electricity; every afternoon I would take off for this apartment armed with my notebooks and pens, thermal underwear, and a bottle of Polish vodka. I would write for two or three hours until my fingers were numb, then return to our smaller but warmer digs. In that cold "loaner" apartment I wrote short stories in longhand into a red notebook; our oven-warmed room I reserved for writing many of the poems that would make up my second book, *Museum.*

As idyllic as those months were, the wet, chilly summer of 1980 primed us for melancholy during a cold and dreary autumn, ten weeks of which we spent lecturing, debating, and writing at the International Working Period for Authors in the city of Bielefeld. By now I noticed a disturbing development: I was losing my English. Not that I couldn't speak fluently or read English as quickly as I had in the past; it was simply that the more fluent my German became, the more insecure I became about what, exactly, constituted "normal" American syntax and cadence whenever I sat down to write poetry. I could no longer locate the precise tone of a phrase, nor gauge the subterranean currents of a line. Prepositions were especially sinister. This terrifyingly subtle process was probably the main reason I had taken so desperately to writing short stories in that borrowed unheated apartment—with prose, the damage was more manageable.

I felt that I had to go back to America. Although he had experienced no such language difficulties during his years in the United States, Fred was immediately sympathetic.

A friend sent me the MLA (Modern Language Association) job list, and I began the onerous procedure of highlighting possible openings, assembling my resume, and writing letters. In February 1981 I flew to the States for interviews; back in Berlin there was another flurry of phone calls before the decision was reached to accept a tenure track position as assistant professor for creative writing at Arizona State University in Tempe, Arizona.

Tempe had put on her best face for my interview in February: mild temperatures and sunny skies, palm trees and balmy breezes. We moved to Arizona in the middle of the summer, driving cross-country from Ohio in a third-hand station wagon. When we pulled our huge black Buick into a rest area just outside Phoenix and I stepped from its air-conditioned interior into the blazing heat of early August, tears popped into my eyes. Valley of the Sun, indeed—this was a cauldron! My skin prickled; I gasped, and the air was as hot and dry as a furnace blast. The pavement heat began to work its way through the thin soles of my sandals, so I ran to the bathroom, the tears drying on my cheeks as quickly as they streamed down. What had I done?

"Don't worry; in a while your blood will thin and you won't feel the heat," Phoenicians (as we took to calling the long-term inhabitants) assured me. And sure enough, by October I had gotten used to drinking mass quantities of fluid, and I actually liked the way the heat made me feel purged and radiant, as crisp as a freshly baked cookie. Dissipating stress was easy: simply lean against a car seat warmed by the sun and all the tension automatically drained from the upper back. People tended to be very friendly Out West: total strangers might touch my arm to emphasize a point when I asked for directions, on the sun-drenched campus everyone smiled as if to make up for the lack of eye contact caused by the ubiquitous dark glasses. Many students were commuters; many worked in order to put themselves through school; many were older and came to class with a fierce desire to learn.

We moved into a spanking new apartment complex that boasted free utilities and instant landscaping. Norman Dubie, senior poet on the faculty, and his wife Jeannine came by with a house plant and helped us carry in a couch, desk, and dinette set that Fred and I had scavenged from local Goodwill and Salvation Army stores. Since I was slated to spend the spring semester at Tuskegee Institute in Alabama as writer-in-residence, we decided to hold off on buying a bed; instead, we spread out our station wagon mattresses (two narrow foam rubber pads we kept for overnight camping trips) on the plushly carpeted bedroom floor and slept on them for those first five months.

Alabama was yet another adjustment. Whereas everything in Tempe was pretty new (the house we would buy a year later boasted the distinction of being located in an "older" neighborhood, all of twenty years old!), Tuskegee Institute seemed not to have changed significantly since Booker T. Washington's time. My classroom flaked paint and exuded mold, and there was a fifteen-inch hole in the linoleum floor, between the pitted oak desk and the cracked blackboard. When I reported it, maintenance came over promptly to patch it by nailing crosshatched two-by-fours over the cavity. All semester I stubbed my toe on the boards as I paced and lectured.

Adequate housing for such a short time could not be found in Tuskegee, which was not much more than a hamlet, so we rented a tiny brick house twenty-five miles away in Auburn. We were cautioned that, though our particular neighborhood (arranged around a circular turnabout) was "safe," we should always check our rear-view mirror when returning home to make sure no one was trailing us. Shocked and a bit incredulous, we soon adopted this useful paranoia when, a week later, we surprised a man trying to slash our tires while we were in the supermarket.

Once Fred and I were driving back from Tuskegee after a dusting of snow had canceled classes. Near Auburn University, in front of a fraternity house "garnished" with a large Confederate flag, we had to slow down in order to pass by throngs of frat boys waging a snowball fight; when they saw who we were, they blocked the street, began hurling snowballs at our car, and screamed epithets I was too scared to actually understand and which Fred was reluctant to repeat to me later. "No way, you bastards!" Fred muttered, and pressed down on the accelerator; when they realized he had no qualms about running them down, the frat boys scattered and we shot through, trailed by snowballs and screams.

The semester in Alabama was my first extended experience living in the South. Our "mixed" marriage had occasioned raised eyebrows or disdaining glances before, but never had we been exposed to such fiercely hateful glares. Every day I would drive the half hour into Tuskegee and meet open, friendly faces;

each evening I would check the rear-view mirror twice before turning into our street. And social climate matched the actual weather: Although the temperatures were cooler than in Arizona, the Alabamian air was more oppressive and, as spring arrived, cloying with the strange sickly sweet odors of the Deep South—wet kudzu, barbecue smoke, and insect repellent.

It was a relief to return to Arizona that August. I soon fell into the rhythm of the laid-back lifestyle—impromptu picnics in the desert and dinner parties where the guests, attired in shorts and loose cottons, congregated around the grill or the pool. When we looked up the daughter of one of our Alabama acquaintances shortly after our return to Tempe, we discovered three intersecting interests: She and I were both four months pregnant, her father was one of America's foremost poets (Hayden Carruth), and we were looking for a house just as she and her husband were trying to sell theirs. We settled the transaction with a minimum of paperwork and moved into our new home in mid-September; the backyard was bursting with figs and olives.

We spent all autumn painting our first own house in bold colors: Pompeiian red walls and royal blue ceiling in the bedroom, pastel blue and yellow for the nursery (the ceiling half blue and half yellow, diagonally), an aubergine-colored foyer and palest pink living room. Colleagues who came to dinner were polite, but we could tell they thought we'd gone bonkers.

I went into labor at four in the morning of January 24, a few hours after painting the bathroom mustard yellow with a coral stripe at chest level. The day before, the midwife had sent me home predicting I wouldn't deliver for another week; depressed, anxious, but determined to put this extra time to use, I hemmed the living room curtains and cleaned out several drawers before tackling the bathroom, unaware that the nesting instinct had kicked in. Thirty-six hours later, Aviva Chantal Tamu Dove-Viebahn was born.

Although I had written very little during the last months of pregnancy, I had felt no anxiety; now the poems began to explode onto the page. While living in Berlin I had begun a group of poems about my grandfather's early adult years: Haunted by a story my grandmother had told me about my grandfather working on a Mississippi riverboat as part of a song-and-dance team, I had written five or six poems revolving around this young man who somehow would become my sweet, shy grandfather. At that point I thought I would be satisfied with a cycle of a half dozen poems; I submitted this grouping to the *Ohio Review*, which had been printing "chapbooks" as centerpieces for each issue. In Alabama, I completed several more "grandfather" poems, so I rearranged the cycle and sent the revised version to *Ohio Review* editor Wayne Dodd with an apology and an explanation; it was this group of poems that appeared as the chapbook "Mandolin" in *Ohio Review* 28.

I was writing every day, driven by the fear of maternal distraction as much as by the elation of creativity. Fred and I had devised a strict schedule in order to ensure working time: One of us would tend Aviva for four hours in the morning, then be relieved for the next four; we allotted two hours for dinner, and then the first sitter would take over again for four more hours. Every day we switched the order. After a week, we realized we had allowed little time for all three of us to be together, so we relaxed the schedule to include one four-hour work period on either side of a four-hour "family time." Also, I had to figure my teaching and related university work into the timetable. A Guggenheim Fellowship allowed me to take a leave of absence the following academic year (1983-84), so we were able to extend our writing schedule.

The modest cycle of "grandfather" poems sent to the *Ohio Review* expanded dramatically one evening when, while giving a poetry reading, I turned to "Dusting," a poem written way back in Berlin and already included in *Museum*:

Every day a wilderness—no
shade in sight. Beulah
patient among knickknacks,
the solarium a rage
of light, a grainstorm
as her gray cloth brings
dark wood to life.

Under her hand scrolls
and crests gleam
darker still. What
was his name, that
silly boy at the fair with
the rifle booth? And his kiss and
the clear bowl with one bright
fish, rippling
wound!

Not Michael—
something finer. Each dust
stroke a deep breath and
the canary in bloom.
Wavery memory: home
from a dance, the front door
blown open and the parlor
in snow, she rushed
the bowl to the stove, watched
as the locket of ice
dissolved and he
swam free.

That was years before
Father gave her up
with her name, years before

her name grew to mean
Promise, then
Desert-in-Peace.
Long before the shadow and
sun's accomplice, the tree.

Maurice.

At this point, with some distance acquired between poem and its original inception, I realized that the room described in it was modeled on my grandmother's solarium, and the woman trying so desperately to recall her first love's name was none other than my grandmother. It was as if she had stepped out of the poem to claim her place in my grandfather's cycle; "you can't tell just one side of a story," she seemed to be saying. In that moment, *Thomas and Beulah* was born: a book-length collection of poems chronicling the lives of my maternal grandparents, an epiphanal series of vignettes depicting an ordinary marriage lived out against the grand panorama of History—the Great Migration of blacks from the rural South to the urban North, world wars and depressions, the civil rights movement and the rise of Afro-American activism in the sixties.

During this blessed time, the poems in *Thomas and Beulah* assembled themselves. I phoned my mother every weekend to talk about her childhood. And although she knew I was writing about her parents, she never asked to see a single poem. Her implicit trust, her faith that I would do justice to their lives, was the most positive force I experienced while writing the book.

Fred's fortieth birthday fell on a Thursday in April of 1987. I had planned a small surprise party, and since I had no classes to teach that day, I informed the English Department that we weren't to be disturbed at home for any reason.

I arose at eleven and kept the shades drawn while I made coffee. According to my secret itinerary, I planned to pick up Aviva from preschool (where Fred had taken her at eight in the morning, before going to bed), drive with her by the shop for the surprise ice-cream cake, special-ordered with a video camera frosted on top—as an amateur photographer with his first video camera, Fred filmed everything that moved. Then we would surprise him before dinner with seven gifts relating to the seven most significant periods of his life. After dinner, our closest friends were scheduled to "drop by" for champagne.

Since I knew we were expecting guests, I had planned to do a bit of surreptitious housecleaning, so I decided to sweep the kitchen floor before Fred got up. The phone rang; I let the answering machine take the call and began to fume when the voice of my department chairman filled the room. What nerve, I thought, I had told them I didn't want to be bothered for anything, banging my broom into a corner as he repeated, a bit frantically, "Rita, I know you're there. Pick up—this is important!"

He had already told me a few weeks earlier that my promotion to full professor had passed all the committees, so what could this be about? Snatching up the receiver, I snarled: "What is it, Nick?" The dialogue that followed was worthy of Laurel and Hardy:

"You've gotten the Pulitzer!"

"No."

"Yes!"

"No!"

"Yes!"

In the end it was the tone of his voice, an octave higher than normal, that convinced me he was telling the truth. I was totally unprepared. What about Fred's surprise party? At that moment, Fred came barreling into the room, eyes popped wide; I must have screamed.

Nick was still talking: ". . . couldn't get hold of you because your number was unlisted so they called the president of the university and *he* didn't have it either, so he had to call me but I told him, no, *I* want to tell her. Listen—the press has started calling here; you don't want them to have your number, do you?"

"No . . ."

"So I'll arrange a press conference for . . . let's say three o'-clock. That should give you enough time to collect yourself. Meet me at the office."

Two hours! What should I wear? And my hair needed washing. And we had to pick up Aviva; what about the cake?

"I don't know how to give a press conference," I wailed into the telephone.

"You'll learn," Nick replied, and hung up.

My hair did not get washed that day. We scooped up Aviva and made our way to the university, where colleagues were waiting with flowers for me and balloons for Aviva. Our friends picked up the video camera cake on their way to our house later that evening, and the surprise party was sprung three hours later than planned, but all the heartier.

Nick was right. One moment I was sweeping the kitchen and the next moment the klieg lights were turned on, and ever since I've been learning the ropes in the strange public arena. The girl who shied away from junior high school play auditions now found herself, when her home town organized a "Rita Dove Day," standing on a stage before an audience of three thousand, talking about her childhood in Akron and reading her poems. The high school senior who had described herself in a personality survey as "dreamy, sensitive, and mild" was now invited for radio interviews and TV talk shows. The young woman who avoided speech classes in college now spoke in front of classrooms and auditoriums nationwide. The bookworm had to learn to dictate letters into a Dictaphone and how to pack a carry-on suitcase for an eight-city tour, how to sleep sitting up and even to be cheerful at 8:00 A.M. breakfasts—by far the most difficult task!

⁓

I had a sabbatical, pre-Pulitzer approved, for 1987-88, and we spent the first half hopscotching all over—from islands off the coast of Yugoslavia (sweltering in June) to the German island of Amrum in the North Sea (near-freezing in July); then came an international poetry festival in Mexico City, followed by four weeks of frenzied writing in Berlin (Aviva went to preschool—called a *Kinderladen* or "children's store"—every day while Fred and I wrote in an architectural firm's spare rooms overlooking Kurfürstendamm, Berlin's "Fifth Avenue."

Late September found us in the States again. Akron's "Rita Dove Day" went nonstop for the first two days in October, with speeches at my old high school, before 650 business women and men at a luncheon, and finally before an audience of 3,000 at the local performance hall which was followed by the signing of over 1,000 books. At the city hall reception, Aviva got her face painted at a clown stand and held her helium balloons in front of the mayor's face as he presented me with the key to the city.   Relatives I hadn't seen since I was twelve stormed the town and ended up in my parents' living room, munching pota-to chips. My fourth grade teacher was telling reporters how I had recited the Preamble to the Constitution, something I don't remember ever being able to do. My fifth grade teacher (the first black teacher I ever had) handed me a term paper I had written back then on the effects of alcoholism. One near-hysterical woman insisted that I had gone to the prom with her son, and when I answered that I hadn't gone to the prom at all (that had been the day Haldeman snapped at us Presidential Scholars in D.C.!) she refused to believe me, brandishing instead a Polaroid snapshot of her son (whom I recognized) posing with a young lady I had never seen before. "See," she exclaimed, "there you are." It was a very bizarre, heart-warming, and frightening experience; I felt like a heroine, a ghost, and a terrible fraud, all at the same time.

From the halls of local history I tumbled into six weeks of deliriously delicious isolation in a borrowed apartment in Paris, where Fred and I (Aviva stayed with her grandmother in Germany) immediately slipped back into our night skins, writing until past 10 A.M., soothed by the ever-changing pulse of the streets in the city that never sleeps. We slept through the dreary wintry afternoons, strolled through the Marais at nightfall, then returned with artichokes and red wine to fuel us again.

In the summer of 1988 I topped off my sabbatical year with a five-week residency at the Rockefeller Foundation's Study and Conference Center in Bellagio, Italy, a pocket of heaven where cypress-covered hills plunge into the clear waters of Lake Como and whitewashed villas slope up into the mists. Perched high on a promontory above the town, the castle-like Villa Serbelloni accommodates more than a dozen scholars and artists at a time, who are expected to work on their specific projects but are often found ambling through the estate along the exquisitely groomed paths, identifying the tiger lily and the hydrangea and the tiniest orchid.

And ah, the villa itself! The only times before that I had walked along such magnificent halls—full of marble niches and four-foot marble urns filled with fresh floral arrangements whose blooms were culled every morning from the villa's own greenhouses—had been behind tour guides.

Meals were opulent, with waiters who would not dream of making a guest reach for the morning coffeepot. Dinner was always a five- to six-course affair, with *aperitivi* served beforehand and menus on creme stationery tucked among the linen napkins, hand-tatted place settings, and silver candlesticks. It was almost too elegant, too beautiful.

Fred and I were assigned a luxurious bedroom in the villa,

and each of us had a more rustic studio in different parts of the grounds. I tried to forge a routine which would allow me to enjoy the culinary delights (and the copious wine selection) without cramping my writing schedule, but I ended up spending most afternoons drowsing in a rattan chair outside my study (actually a one-story tower without a castle, a stone cylinder set at the top of a grassy knoll with windows looking out on all four directions, like a lighthouse), watching the three goldfish in my private little lily pond. Gradually I ceased feeling guilty about doing nothing (i.e., not writing) and learned the deep pleasure of simply *being*:

AND COUNTING
(Bellagio, Italy)

Well of course I'm not worth it but neither is
the Taj Majal for that matter so who's counting?
Someone's got to listen to the fountain;
someone is due to catch the *nymphaea tuberosa*
closing promptly five till five. Opulence
breathes on its own a little better
if there's a gardener raking or a scholar
primed to record its suscitation. I came here

to write, knock a few poems off the ledger
of accounts payable—only to discover
pasta put me under just as neatly as sambuca
would catapult me into telepathic communication. So
I took a few day trips, sprained an ankle on the courts,
fell asleep over Catullus-*cum*-Zukofsky . . . in

short, nothing happened that wasn't unexceptional,
but that's the crux of moral implication, is it not?
Mother Mary, ingénue with the golden womb,
you would not comprehend how cruel a modern game of

tennis is: you only had one phosphorescent ball.

Here's a riddle for Our Age: when the sky's the limit, how can you tell you've gone too far?

⌒

Each autumn upon returning to Arizona from summer vacation, my allergies had worsened. Contrary to popular belief, Arizona—particularly the heavily populated areas—is no longer a haven for hay-fever sufferers. Homesick easterners moving into the Sun Belt often bring their cherished gardens and lawns with them; this maddening practice, which also requires obsessive watering, as well as the large number of swimming pools in the Greater Phoenix area, have resulted in high levels of pollen and dry mold. My allergy problems, plus my yearning for seasonal changes, first prompted me to consider the offer of a position at the University of Virginia. After many tortured months of discussion and soul-searching we decided to pull up stakes, moving first to Durham, North Carolina, where I was a fellow at the National Humanities Center for the 1988-89 academic year. And finally, in August 1989, we moved into our dream house just outside of Charlottesville—window seats and fireplaces, windows upon windows looking out on our lake and trees and the Blue Ridge Mountains in the distance.

We never regretted the decision. The university grounds are beautiful, the faculty and students everything one could wish for in an academic setting. And as far as spiritual energy is concerned, a marvelous *frisson* results from the way the Jeffersonian legacy of the "academic village" is superimposed on the high-tech, light-industry infrastructure of the town; the more recent influx of progressive academics, avant-garde artists, reclusive Hollywood connections, the "horse set," and the multimillion-aire set all add intriguing flavors to the cultural gumbo. Hard to imagine that a mere twenty-five to thirty years ago this university was a fortress of racism and male chauvinism!

Aviva's horseback riding lessons (part of the bargain struck to persuade her to move away from Arizona) have turned her into quite a horsewoman; Fred plays squash and plugs away at his first American novel. I continue the singing lessons begun in Durham and occasionally venture onto the stage of the University Opera Workshop.

The perverse thing about fame is that the more recognition there is, the less time remains to continue doing that for which one has been recognized. Since the Pulitzer Prize, it seems that my daily life has become a struggle against fragmentation; carving out the necessary blocks of time in which to write has become increasingly difficult. The requests for appearances and interviews, book reviews and essays, promotional comments and letters of recommendation keep pouring in; even to answer with a polite "no" demands an extraordinary amount of time. Being a responsible and "present" mother is important to me: I have turned down trips to China and France and writing residencies in beautiful places because it would have meant being absent from home for undue periods; my pleasures are taken in the homey and intimate delights of the everyday, the miracles of the ordinary.

Life continues in its fits and starts superimposed over the comfort of dailiness. Not a day goes by that I don't curse the telephone and the Federal Express truck bringing more urgent requests and unsolicited manuscripts; but not a day passes that I don't look out over the hills and think, "What a charmed place this is; how lucky I am to live in it."

I had thought, when the initial brouhaha of the Pulitzer had trickled away, that at least never again in my life would I be *that* surprised. But two days after the announcement that I had been appointed the new Poet Laureate of the United States, I was driving home from the university, and the thought hit me: "Damn," I said aloud, "it happened again." I know now not to wager bets against fate. More and more often these days I am reminded of the advice my father gave me—repeated in a few prophetic lines in my sonnet "Flash Cards":

In math I was the whiz kid, keeper
of oranges and apples. *What you don't understand,*
master, my father said; the faster
I answered, the faster they came.

I could see one bud on the teacher's geranium,
one clear bee sputtering at the wet pane.
The tulip trees always dragged after heavy rain
so I tucked my head as my boots slapped home.

My father put up his feet after work
and relaxed with a highball and *The Life of Lincoln.*
After supper we drilled and I climbed the dark

before sleep, before a thin voice hissed
numbers as I spun on a wheel. I had to guess.
Ten, I kept saying, *I'm only ten.*

Life and work are coming at me fast and furious these days, so I'm happy I received such good training in flash cards. I'm grateful to all the mentors (parents, relatives, neighbors, teachers, students, husband, and daughter) who have shown me by example that life is only worth writing about if one is really living it. I take the "slings and arrows of outrageous fortune" as they come, and write between the interstices.

∾ *p o s t s c r i p t :*

One of those super-successful computer whiz kids once said: "I can't believe my life is happening to me." When Richard Nixon's telegram arrived at my parents' house nearly a quarter century ago, I felt the estranging power of good fortune. Looking back, it seems like I must have been sleepwalking through the media blitz following the Pulitzer Prize; the charmed weeks in Bellagio are now no more substantial than a trail of smoke rings. And when the phone rang that morning in May 1993 in my Chicago hotel room where I was packing for the return trip after a two-day reading and panel event with Gwendolyn Brooks—when the voice on the other end of the line asked if I would consider becoming Poet Laureate of the United States, it was only training and Nick's statement "You'll learn" that enabled me to formulate a more or less coherent response. The weeks that followed were ten times more strenuous than those after the Pulitzer, but I learned to handle the publicity with a measure of calm—all the while feeling like I was a piece in some Titan's chess game, a Queen run amok, certain to be decapitated with the next move. This sense of unreality, of fickle fortune, helped me survive those first weeks—that, plus the unshakable fact that we held nonrefundable plane tickets for mid-June to Europe, where we had already rented a motor home to camp through Scandinavia. Everything—print, radio, and television interviews, photo shoots, pressing correspondence, plus organizing the fall season for the Library of Congress reading series (my first official duty)—had to be finished by mid-June. Remembering my grandmother's advice to *Just do your best and then stop worrying about it,* I plowed through. Upon my return from a rejuvenating month in Norway, Finland, and Sweden (no crowds or reporters, just fiords and reindeer and the midnight sun as available light for reading through piles of books), the mounds of letters towered even higher. But whenever I approached the point of collapse, I would run across a correspondent who had enclosed clippings of her favorite poems (not her own!), or someone who simply wanted to tell me how poetry had enriched his life. This enthusiastic and abiding love for poetry, as expressed by nonacademics, by "people," energized me.

On October 7, 1993, I opened the literary season at the Library of Congress in Washington, D.C., with a poetry reading. The event was held in the Great Hall of the Jefferson Building—hundreds of people crammed into every gilt and marble-adorned corner; closed-circuit televisions were set up between the fluted columns for those standing in the back. I would have been terrified if my grandmother hadn't been beside me in spirit, chuckling, "Now, ain't this nothing!" After the reading, Fred and I were whisked up to the Poetry Office, on the top floor of the same building, in order to change for a black-tie dinner at the White House. As I flung off my reading outfit and stepped into my evening gown, the girl who had wept because nobody had asked her to the high school prom and who had been saved from mortification by being invited as a Presidential Scholar to visit the White House on the same weekend as that prom—this girl had to chuckle, too. It was happening, whether I chose to believe it or not. Outside the balcony windows of the Poetry Office, the dome of the U.S. Capitol glowed like a perfectly turned meringue.

(November 1993)

≈ *a c k n o w l e d g m e n t s*

"Lady Freedom among Us" was read at the ceremony commemorating the 200th anniversary of the United States Capitol and the restoration of the Statue of Freedom to the Capitol dome on October 23, 1993, and first published in the *Congressional Record* of the same day. In the fall of 1994, Janus Press of West Burke, Vermont, issued a limited edition fine press printing of the poem, commissioned by the University of Virginia Libraries as the four millionth volume in their collections.

Rita Dove's "Autobiography" was first published in the *Contemporary Authors Autobiography Series,* vol. 19 (Detroit: Gale Research Inc., 1994).

Poem by Nadia Tuéni from *Poèmes pour une histoire* (Paris: Seghers, 1966) is reprinted by permission of Editions Seghers.

"Song to a Negro Wash-woman" by Langston Hughes reprinted from *Golden Slippers,* edited by Arna Bontemps (New York: Harper & Row, c 1941), is reprinted by permission of Harold Ober Associates, Inc.